PENGU

BACK
TO THE
LAND

Lynda Hallinan is editor-at-large of *NZ Gardener*
magazine. In 2007 she made an ambitious (some might
say nutty) New Year's resolution to spend 12 months
living self-sufficiently in the city, growing all her own
food in her 733-square metre Auckland garden. In 2010,
having met her soon-to-be husband, Jason, she started all
over again on a 20-hectare property 45 minutes from the
city. Lynda is a keen gardener, pickler, brewer, frustrated
florist and a regular stallholder at the Clevedon Village
Farmers' Market. *Back to the Land* follows her journey for
12 months and includes tales from her weekly column in
the *Sunday Star-Times' Sunday* magazine, and her blog,
www.lyndahallinan.com.

Back
to the
Land

A Year of
Country
Gardening

Lynda Hallinan

Photography by **Sally Tagg**

PENGUIN BOOKS

CONTENTS

For my grandmother, Pat,
the original domestic goddess.

For my parents, Jock and Marjorie.
I appreciate everything you've done for me,
and everything you still do.

For my big sister, Brenda. Thanks for raising the
alarm when, aged two, I tried to pat a frog, fell
into a cattle trough and almost drowned.

For my husband, Jason.
You'll always be my Hunk from Hunua.

And for Lucas. One day all this will be yours.
If your country childhood is half as much fun
as mine was, you're in for one hell of a ride.

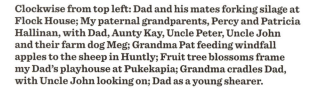

Clockwise from top left: Dad and his mates forking silage at
Flock House; My paternal grandparents, Percy and Patricia
Hallinan, with Dad, Aunty Kay, Uncle Peter, Uncle John
and their farm dog Meg; Grandma Pat feeding windfall
apples to the sheep in Huntly; Fruit tree blossoms frame
my Dad's playhouse at Pukekapia; Grandma cradles Dad,
with Uncle John looking on; Dad as a young shearer.

THE WOMEN IN MY FAMILY HAVE A HABIT OF MARRYING FARMERS. My paternal grandmother, Patricia Earl, now in her 95th year, has outlived not one but two farming husbands. I have both men to thank for my rural roots; one for my genes, the other for the farm, midway between Auckland and Hamilton, where I was raised.

Grandma Pat grew up in Raglan and, at 19, took up a position as governess for a farming family at Awaroa Bay on Waiheke Island. She'd no sooner set foot on the wharf than she caught the eye of a young fellow from Hastings, Percy Hallinan. Percy was employed as a scrub cutter – a job that attracted an official government subsidy – though he was actually working covertly as a shepherd.

In 1939, newly wed and with a new baby, my grandmother started a diary. For 73 years she has written in it every week, though her eyesight's failing these days and, by the sound of it, so too her resolve. She's forgotten why she started it.

'Perhaps so I could write down what a wonderful baby [her eldest son] Peter was,' she chuckles. The first entry reveals her excitement that he'd cut his first tooth.

When Grandma started her diary, she and Percy were living on a farm at Te Rahu, near Te Awamutu, and she faithfully recorded the minutiae of life as a farmer's wife. She wrote of lamb drafts and ewes in need of drenching; making plum jam and preserving eggs for winter; sewing clothes and curtains; bottling beans and nectarines.

In 1943 my father, Jock, was born and Percy was offered a job managing a Huntly farm owned by a wealthy Auckland land agent.

'The farm,' Grandma wrote, 'of 300 odd acres (121 hectares), has 500 sheep and 70 cattle running on it and is mostly peat swamp. The house doesn't look much from the outside but by all accounts will be very nice inside, all electric, so I'll be really flash.'

The family spent the next 20 years in that cottage on Pukekapia Road. Grandma raised four boys, a daughter and countless stray cats, while Percy grew his beloved gladioli and planted more than 50 fruit trees – 'Golden Queen' peaches, 'Gravenstein' apples and every type of plum bar 'Greengage'. Grandma has an old aerial photograph that shows the house all but obscured in a cloud of marshmallow-pink blossom. (Sadly, though the house is unchanged, someone took a chainsaw to the orchard in the intervening years. Not one of those fruit trees still stands.)

Grandma's diary is notably short on sentiment, even when, in February 1965, the peat bog she described as 'the curse of the Waikato' claimed my grandfather's life.

'I've got to drive myself to write. Somehow I feel that when I do this, these events are irrevocable. I still can't take in properly what has happened. Percy was drowned when the tractor overturned and pinned him in the main drain on February 12. It was pelting with rain and we didn't know how it happened as he was on his own. The funeral was on Monday morning at the Crematorium, a private affair, no flowers and the minimum of fuss, which is what Percy wanted.'

Percy wouldn't have wanted her to mope, she says, so she busied herself bottling fruit. In the days after his death she wrote, 'I have been trying to get on with some preserving but it's hard. I just don't want to. However I got five jars of apples done yesterday and two jars of blackberries. I've done 18 jars of plums off the late plum tree, four of beans and 19 of tomatoes.'

A year after Percy's death, Grandma moved off the farm at Pukekapia Road and went flatting with my Aunty Kay in Auckland. Soon after, she rekindled her friendship with an Onewhero dairy farmer by the name of Evan Glasgow, also recently widowed. Grandma and Evan had known each other since 1929 when, as founding pupils of the Correspondence School's Secondary Department, they were encouraged to become penpals. Grandma wrote to Evan and he wrote back because, as she'd signed her name Pat, he'd assumed she was a boy.

Evan was a shy country lad who was slow to make a move. When he went off to war, serving in North Africa and Italy, he optimistically carried Grandma's photo in his pocket ... only to return home to the news that she'd already married someone else.

Who says unrequited love is a lost cause? My grandparents married and merged families in 1967 and in 1974 – the year I was born – my new granddad retired to the Thames coast and sold his farm to my father.

My maternal grandmother was no traditional country bride.

Clarice McIlroy graduated from Victoria University in 1931 with a Master's Degree in English, which didn't prove particularly useful for bagging a bloke. Seven years later, staring firmly down the barrel of spinsterhood, she answered a newspaper advert placed by my grandfather, Albert Cornes.

Albert was a dairy farmer from Te Mata, in the backblocks of Raglan, where the Cornes family name is as old as the district. He'd inherited the family farm from his father John Cornes, who married my great-grandmother, Mary McPherson, in 1876. Mary's brother had fought in the Land Wars and was granted a 395-acre (160-hectare) bush block in the shadow of Mount Karioi. The story goes that Captain McPherson rode his horse out from Hamilton but got only as far as the

Whatawhata Deviation before he couldn't be fagged riding further, so he gifted the land to his sister.

Albert must have admired Clarice's penmanship, for he proposed by return post, sending a piece of paper with holes cut out of it (so he could size up her finger for the ring). Her mother (my great-grandmother Susannah) was not amused. 'A farmer,' she sniffed snootily, 'is only one step up from a shopkeeper.'

In his defence, Albert was no intellectual slouch. He was a bachelor with a house full of books, a crossword fanatic, a photographer and a musician. He played both banjo and violin until an unfortunate incident in the cow shed – he caught his hand in the chain drive of the cream separator – claimed the tips of two of his fingers.

Albert was 43 and Clarice 30 when they married at her parents' home in Feilding. Back in Te Mata, six children followed in quick succession, including my mother, Marjorie.

Clarice had no choice but to adapt to country life: she joined the Women's Division of the Federated Farmers, churned her own butter, kept Black Orpington hens and Khaki Campbell ducks, reared calves and fattened her own pigs. She also hoped for more for her daughters, who disappointed her terribly when they chose shearers and pig hunters as prospective husbands.

Mum didn't marry a farmer – she married a farming school dropout.

Well, to be fair, Dad didn't drop out. He was expelled from the agricultural training college at Flock House in Bulls a fortnight before he was due to graduate in 1960. He and his mate Keith got into a spot of bother when the superintendent caught them hiding booze in the bushes; both boys scarpered but Dad tripped, smashing a bottle of beer in his pocket. He was caught red-handed (or in this case, bloody-trousered with beer-bottle fragments in his thigh) and dismissed in disgrace.

Clockwise from top left: My maternal grandparents, Albert and Clarice Cornes on their wedding day; Grandma Pat and Granddad Evan at Mum and Dad's wedding; Albert Cornes was a keen photographer – he took this self-portrait; My great-grandparents, John and Mary Cornes (at rear of carriage); My grandparents sent their cream to the Raglan Dairy Co-op; Clearing the bush on the farm at Te Mata.

Clockwise from top left: Mum reared the calves at Onewhero (Dad didn't have the patience, she says); Dad dismantled an old reel lawnmower and rebuilt it as this motorbike; Me and my pet lamb, Cindy II, at Calf Club Day, 1980; Me and Brenda with her lamb, Mary I, at Calf Club Day, 1978; Mum and one of her mighty Waikato cauliflowers. I'm responsible for the slight baby bump. Opposite page: Me, Brenda and our friend Jenny Walter with our lambs Cindy I, Mary II and Scamper.

Dad arrived back at Pukekapia Road shame-faced but quite good at shearing. He bought his first hand-piece – it cost 12 pound 10 shillings – and teamed up with a mate to service local sheep farms. On his best day, he did 456 ewes.

Mum was working as a draughtswoman, drawing maps for the Lands and Survey Department in Hamilton, when their paths crossed at a party in 1967. When Mum took Dad home to meet her parents, Clarice took one look at this loquacious, hollow-legged Huntly shearer and tried to put a stop to it. 'If you keep going out with him,' she told Mum, 'you won't

meet anyone better.' What did Albert think? His wryly astute verdict is true of all Hallinans. 'Well, he's not lost for words,' he said.

My parents married in Te Mata, bought a little brick house in Hamilton, put in a garden and grew some fine cauliflowers. My sister, Brenda, was born in 1973 and I arrived exactly one year later. Then, when I was six weeks old, my parents sold up in suburbia, signed up for a rural bank loan and shifted to Onewhero (a place so blink-and-you'll-miss-it that you can rearrange the letters to spell O Nowhere) to take over Granddad's 89-acre (36-hectare) dairy farm.

Dad freely admits he had no idea how to run a farm. He went to Dairy Discussion Group meetings – a monthly cow cocky catch-up more critical than a clutch of coffee-group mums – and was too embarrassed to ask any questions.

It was hard going: my parents made $1500 in their first year as farmers. We didn't have much, but we wanted for nothing. Except, perhaps, a horse. (We were never allowed one – apparently a horse eats as much grass as seven cows – though Mum and Dad did relent one year and let us borrow our neighbour Mr Tully's Shetland pony. Neddy was a short, surly adversary who would sooner bite your hand than take the carrot in it. After a week we were happy to hand the reins back.)

We had a TV, but we didn't watch it much. We were too busy building huts in the trees; foraging for wild blackberries; playing Go Home, Stay Home with the Massey kids next door; picnicking in the paddocks; making dams in the ditches; scoffing stolen feijoas; making grass-blade whistles and potato guns; raising Calf Club champion calves and chubby pet lambs; turning Milo tins into pinhole cameras; and scaring the wits out of each other with wetas from the woodshed.

It was a chocolate-box country childhood but, as a know-it-all teen, I moved to Auckland to study journalism, was instantly seduced by the city . . . and had no intention to ever go back to the land.

Top left: Our first portrait as a farming family, on the verandah in Onewhero, 1974; Bottom left: Me and Moozi, 1986; Right: My sister and me with our prize-winning pet calves, Sparkle and Patsy, at Calf Club Day in 1982. Opposite page: Mr and Mrs Hinton on our wedding day. Lucas is there too, disguised behind the biggest bouquet of dahlias I could feasibly carry.

My husband isn't technically a farmer though, at 6 foot 4, nor can he be accurately described as a smallholder.

Jason is a civil engineering contractor who grew up in suburban west Auckland. Graham Henry (now 'Sir') was his headmaster at Kelston Boys High School. Fifteen years ago he bought a 20-hectare block at Hunua, on Auckland's south-east fringe, but he's a Westie at heart. I've seen the photographic evidence from his teenage years: skin-tight leather pants; skinny tie; blond mullet; AC/DC posters on the wall.

Although a townie through and through, Jason spent his summer holidays on his grandparents' 10-hectare block at Waipipi, near Waiuku on Franklin's west coast. Fred and Adeline (Addie) Hinton could outdo Barbara and Tom Good: they appear in the archives of the *Franklin County News* proudly showing off a 3kg kumara.

Fred was a practical man who taught his grandsons how to harrow fields, rake hay and net flounder in the mudflats along the farm's coastal boundary. He brewed his own stout and cider – his old apple press now has pride of place in our barn – and grew everything from thornless blackberries and purple-podded Dutch capucijner peas to speckled Yugoslav beans. (Some days I wish he hadn't been such a skilled gardener. 'But that's not how Grandpa used to do it,' my husband mutters when I don't space my spuds or stake my beans correctly.)

My grandmother Clarice had to resort to a personal ad to meet her husband, whereas I fell for mine – literally – at the Drury Rugby Club. The night we met, at a 50th birthday party for some bloke my brother-in-law knows, I slipped in a spilt beer – not my own, I hasten to add – and broke my wrist.

Did Jason have any inkling what he was in for, entering into a relationship with a gung-ho gardener with a big gob? Possibly. Under threat of death (or worse, being dumped on the eve of my 35th birthday), I was ordered never to mention his name in print. From then on, he was known in my *Sunday Star-Times* columns simply as The Hunk from Hunua.

Two weeks after we met, I ordered 100 heirloom fruit trees for his front paddock. Two months on, I gave him six Pekin ducks to fatten for the Christmas table. And two years to the day after we met, we welcomed our son Lucas into the world.

When I left the country for the city, I vowed I'd never again find myself at the back end of a cow. And yet, here I am, at home on the Hunua Ranges, with a pantry full of preserves, a shed full of rough cider and home-brewed hop beer, 26 cattle, 12 ewes, a geriatric ram called Rambo, his challenger Night Rider, 13 chooks, four cats and two dogs.

My high heels are gathering dust, there's an ever-increasing stack of *NZ Lifestyle Block* magazines by my bed, and I've just bought a new shopping bag to take to the Clevedon Farmers' Market on Sundays. It's nothing like the luxury leather Kenzo bag from Paris I used to tote; it's eco-friendly cotton with three big green words stamped on the front. It says, 'Rural and Proud'.

lynda hallinan

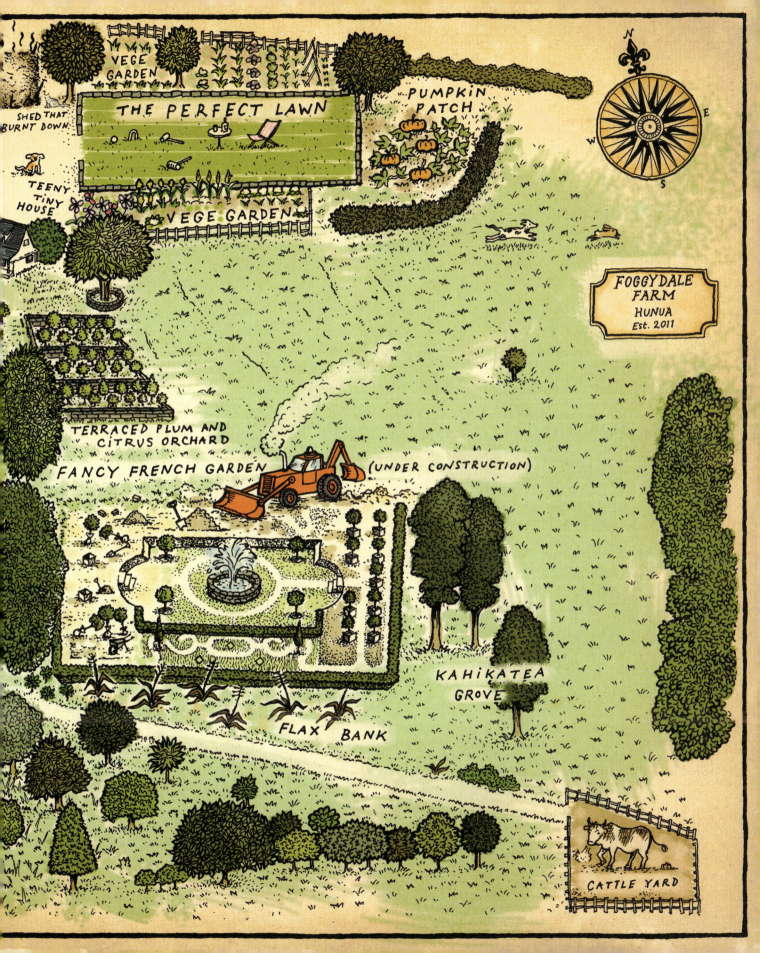

WINTER

The landscape is laid bare. This is the season of sombre skies, sullen stock, skeletal trees, Swanndris and wet woollen socks.

Mr Puppy Doo-Hawg

WINTER IS A WAITING GAME ON OUR FARM.

We're waiting for the cows to run out of grass; for the braided rivers of mud snaking through our paddocks to link limbs and swallow the swamp; for my bare-root fruit trees to be delivered; for Jack Frost to decapitate the last dahlias; and for the birth of our first child.

JUNE 1, 2011: It's only the first day of winter and already I'm counting the days till spring. It's so wet. It's wetter than Marti Pellow. The rain doesn't so much fall in sheets in Hunua as descend in soggy duvets. Our Pekin ducks are delirious but the dogs are downcast, our chooks are sulking, the sheep are solemn and the cows have had a gutsful. They'd rather sit on their hay than eat it.

Our small farm – 20 hectares of what real estate agents euphemistically describe as rolling country – is 125m above sea level, 53km from central Auckland, in the region's far south-east corner. (Having ceremoniously bid farewell to the city in favour of Franklin County, I find bloody Rodney Hide is shifting the boundaries to claim me back.) The average annual rainfall here is 1250mm and almost half will fall before my daffodils bloom. That's if the bulbs don't rot in the sodden soil.

We share our skyline with the Hunua Ranges, home to the rare kokako, the native Hochstetter's frog and four huge catchment dams that keep the taps trickling in Auckland. The largest of those dams, the Mangatangi Reservoir, holds 37 million cubic metres of water; 100,000 cubic metres gush out every day. But that's enough talk of water. I'm impatient for mine to break.

JUNE 2: Our son is due any day. We've already named him Lucas, the only boy's name Jason and I can agree on. We're still debating what to call our farm.

My friend Nadene, who lives down the valley in Mangatawhiri, has called her smallholding Manawa Farm. It translates as 'place of the heart'. Hunua apparently means infertile lands, but as I fell pregnant within two months of moving here, clearly that's bollocks.

It feels rude not to name our place. I've been looking to the landscape for inspiration, but have so far found our farm wanting. There's a grove of kahikatea, a massive weather-beaten macrocarpa and a block of pines between the hill paddocks, but we're still a few oaks short of a forest. We have a rather nice waterfall and a willow-lined wetland, plus dingles, dells and dales, gullies, gorges and swales – and lots of rocks. My husband spent months gouging boulders out of the hills to build the drystone walls, now clothed in a chartreuse winter coat of moss, along our driveway. (No prizes for guessing why his company's called Stonedale Civil.)

Our home is no help either. A two-storey gabled timber house, it's too cramped to be a country chateau or modern manor, but not cute enough to be called a cottage. It's perched on a hilltop plateau that, on chilly mornings, is surrounded on all sides by fog. It rolls up the valley and settles around the shoulders of my vege garden like a shrug.

During my first winter here, I found the fog quite creepy, like the malevolent smog in Stephen King's horror novella *The Mist*, but it's as much a part of this place as the rain and the ravines. So, Foggydale Farm it is.

Lucas and I pictured here six weeks later

JUNE 4: Our stock agent Lyn dropped by this week to assess the steers we're sending to the sale. He took one look at my bloated belly and another at our breeding herd (if you can call one mellow old Jersey and two wild-eyed Murray Greys a herd) and predicted a photo finish as to who'll spot the stork first.

JUNE 6: Two down, two to go. The Murray Greys have both shown me up, delivering two freckle-faced gangly girls, with no medical intervention required – much to the relief of my mother. She was roped into a midwifery role last year and found herself at the business end of the scattiest beast, up to her armpit in afterbirth.

The Jersey girl's bulging undercarriage is matched by a swollen udder hanging halfway to her hooves. She sways from side to side as she hightails it up the hill for some hay, but at least she can still break into a trot. I can't even see my toes, though I did manage to sow a packet of 'Wiltshire Ripple' sweet peas in trays today, while Mum took pity on the cauliflower seedlings languishing in my propagating house, and planted them out.

JUNE 7: Lucas Sebastian Hinton arrived at 10.11 am by emergency caesarean. He's a strapping wee chap, weighing in at 4.47kg (9lb 14oz). Mother and baby both well, though after 24 hours of labour we're both looking a bit worse for wear. We'll wait a few weeks before we invite Sally Tagg down to the farm to take our first proper family portrait.

JUNE 12: I arrived home from the hospital to an email inbox overflowing with indignation. We packed our old bull off to the sale a fortnight ago and I made the mistake of writing about it in my *Sunday Star-Times* column today. Irate animal activists are now accusing me of being a greedy, grubby farmer.

I hadn't been to a cattle sale in two decades, so I was pleased to report that the standard of the Tuakau sale yard's cheese and tomato toasted sandwiches, not to mention their raspberry sticky buns, hadn't slipped a bit in the interim. Our seven black steers cracked the half-tonne and fetched $970 each, while our bull, a foul-tempered, anti-Ferdinand, sold for $1880. He's 740kg of prime hamburger now.

That's life on a farm. Today's lambs are tomorrow's lamb chops; this winter's calves will be spring's Wiener schnitzel. It doesn't pay to get too sentimental about it. Even Michael Pollan, the influential food activist and author of *The Omnivore's Dilemma*, isn't anti-abattoir. As he said on *Oprah*, 'There are farms, and more of them all the time, where animals lead very happy lives . . . and have one bad day.'

That's no comfort to Vivienne, a particularly vociferous vegetarian from Wellington. She calls me a murderer and urges me to keep my cruel thoughts to myself. I write back to her, politely, before thawing a chunk of home-killed beef for dinner. I'm serving a Sunday roast, with all the trimmings, in her honour.

JUNE 14: It's my birthday. I've directed Jason to a jewellery store, as we don't need any more appliances. Last year he gave me his grandfather's cider press. For Christmas I got a KitchenAid mixer and a lime green toaster (to match the wallpaper in our kitchen). I trumped that on his birthday, presenting him with a sausage stuffer . . . and a hank of salted sheep's intestines from the local butcher.

How many sausages does a hank make? How long is a piece of string? The tangled bundle of brined guts now lurking in our beer fridge appears to have no end.

Yorkshire puddings

Yorkshire puddings

I make individual Yorkshire puddings in muffin trays. Combine 1 heaped cup flour and ½ teaspoon salt in a bowl. Break in 2 large eggs, add ½ cup milk and ¼ cup cold water. Beat into a smooth batter and chill in the fridge while the meat cooks. Drain the excess dripping from your roasting tray, add a spoonful of fat to each muffin tin, return to the oven until it's smoking hot, then spoon in the batter and bake at 200°C for 15 minutes, until the puddings are plump and puffy. Then drown 'em in gravy.

The first time we made sausages, it took two hours of shoving, stuffing and swivelling to make a dozen chubby chipolatas. Making the filling was easy – to every 500g minced beef or pork, we added 60g fresh breadcrumbs, 1 beaten egg and 2–3 tablespoons finely chopped herbs – but getting it to feed into the casings was a comedy of errors. It wasn't until I watched an episode of *Masterchef Australia* that I realised where we

were going wrong. The meat needs to be well chilled or it clogs up the auger.

It's my sister's birthday today too. We usually head for the hills – the Bombay Hills – to dine at Bracu restaurant at the Simunovich Olive Estate, but with a one-week-old baby, I'd rather stay in with a plate of homemade bangers and a pile of creamy mashed spud. 'Agria' potatoes, of course.

Our homemade sausages

Horseradish sauce

Horseradish sauce

Roast beef isn't the same without a big spoonful of homegrown horseradish on the side. With foliage that's the spitting image of weedy dock, horseradish (*Armoracia rusticana*) is a vigorous herb with tenacious, tentacle-like roots. Be prepared for a fight come harvest time; it hangs on for dear life. Like mint, it's best planted in a deep pot (a half wine barrel is ideal) or it will colonise your garden.

Method: Scrub or peel the roots and blitz in a food processor or blender. Or finely grate the pallid flesh; do this outdoors or be prepared for tears. Add a splash of cider vinegar, a sprinkle of sugar, and a dollop of whipped cream, crème fraîche or, if you want to keep it in the fridge for more than a few days, sweetened condensed milk. And if you suffer from hay fever, swallow a tablespoonful neat every day. It soon sorts out stuffy sinuses.

JUNE 18: Before I had Lucas, my friend Debbie shared her postnatal wisdom. 'Keep your biscuit tins full,' she advised, so I've been baking cinnamon brioche. Helen Jackson from the Foodlovers website gave me the recipe. Helen makes large, deliciously doughy rolls, but in the interests of shifting my blancmange-like, post-baby belly, I bake mini brioche by the dozen.

Making bread might seem a bit bothersome but it's actually remarkably compatible with caring for a newborn. While the dough's rising there's just enough time to bathe the baby, wash a load of laundry, fetch the mail, feed the chooks, pat the dogs, get out of my pyjamas (if I'm really organised) and slam another casserole into the slow cooker.

'There are reasons why women have learned to multitask and be wonderfully efficient and productive in short spaces of time,' Taranaki plantswoman Abbie Jury told me this week. 'Those reasons are babies.'

JUNE 20: Heather Cole from Mapua Country Trading must be psychic. She sent me a box of loot this morning: booties for Lucas, a bag of dog soap (I suspect she can smell Gypsy and Mr Puppy Doo-Hawg's dank coats from there) and a bag of 'Wilson's Wonder' walnuts. The nuts are as big as mountain oysters, though rather less painful to crack. My mate Rachel can split them open with her bare hands.

MAKING BREAD MIGHT SEEM BOTHERSOME BUT IT'S ACTUALLY REMARKABLY COMPATIBLE WITH CARING FOR A NEWBORN

Helen's cinnamon brioche

Combine 1½ teaspoons active yeast, 1 tablespoon sugar and ½ cup warm milk in a small bowl and set aside in a warm spot till the yeast froths. Lightly whisk 2 egg yolks and 1 egg; add to yeast mixture. Sift 2 cups flour into a large bowl (if your eggs are larger than a size 6, you'll need more flour). Make a well in the centre and pour in the yeast mixture, along with 75g softened butter. Mix into a soft dough, tip onto a floured board and knead until smooth and elastic (about 10 minutes). Place in a greased bowl, cover with a tea towel and pop in your hot water cupboard for an hour, until the dough doubles in size.

Preheat oven to 180°C. Roll out dough into a 20cm x 40cm rectangle, sprinkle with 1 teaspoon cinnamon and ¾ cup brown sugar, and roll up into a log. Slice into pinwheels, brush tops with egg and bake in large muffin tins for 15–20 minutes.

Yesterday Jason planted a pair of grafted 'Wilson's Wonder' trees between the oaks beside our lawn. In time their splendid limbs will plug the gap where the prevailing sou'westerly hurdles over the hill.

Hopefully, they'll also lure the rats out of our chook run. When Jason moved our henhouse last week he found a rat the size of a small cat holed up in a cosy burrow beneath it. Having slyly fashioned a rammed earth basement, the crafty bugger had chewed an egg-sized hole through the floor of one of the nesting boxes for room service.

Heather has also given me her mum Jill's pickled onion recipe, though it feels sacrilege to stray from my family's method. Mum makes a pickling solution of 1 cup brown sugar, 2 litres malt vinegar and 2 tablespoons pickling spice, which she simmers for 15 minutes then cools and pours over onions that have been brined overnight. The first time I made them on my own, I boiled the liquid so hard that it reduced by half, resulting in alarmingly spicy, not to mention ferociously flatulence-inducing, onions.

It's time to sow onions, though with 10kg sacks of 'Pukekohe Longkeeper' onions for sale at our local fruit store for just $10, it hardly seems worth the effort to raise them from seed. Mine always turn out tiddly, so this winter I'm only sowing petite pink 'Tropea Rossa Lunga' and 'Borettana', purely for pickling.

Pickled onions

'Wilson's Wonder'

Jill's pickled onions

Soak small peeled onions overnight in a brine made from 1½ cups plain salt dissolved in 2 litres water. The next day, drain and dry onions. Pack into clean jars with 6–8 peppercorns per jar. Combine 750ml malt vinegar and 500g honey in a pot and heat till the honey has melted. Cool (this step is essential to avoid limp pickles) and pour over onions. Seal jars and leave for at least 14 days before eating.

JUNE 22: It's the shortest day of the year, which means it's time to plant garlic. I'm under strict doctor's instructions to take it easy – no driving, heavy lifting or housework for the next six weeks – but my obstetrician said nothing about getting my fingers back into the soil. And I can't think of a better way to celebrate the winter solstice than with a goblet of mulled wine in one hand and a bag of seed garlic in the other.

When I was growing up, I thought only bearded hippies from Coromandel – and my organic-gardening aunt and uncle in Pukekohe – ate garlic, let alone grew it. My parents were culinary conservatives. We ate meat and three veges, of which potato was always one, every night. I was in high school before I ever ate pasta (if boiled mince and tomato purée slopped over spaghetti counts as authentic bolognese) and my father still mutters if we serve him rice.

My father-in-law, Rex, is no fan of garlic either so my mother-in-law, Maureen, steers clear of it. My husband reckons he'd never seen a raw garlic clove until he met me.

I grew my first, and best, crop of garlic from the purple-skinned seed cloves that my late Uncle John gave me about 15 years ago. How I wish I hadn't eaten it all; good strains of seed garlic are so hard to come by.

Every year I save the fattest cloves from my biggest bulbs to replant. I'm slowly building up my stock of 'Takahue', a Kiwi heirloom discovered growing wild in sand dunes near Ahipara by Koanga Institute founder Kay Baxter. But the kudos for my best garlic goes to Carterton gardener Rosalind Broadmore. Roz and her husband Derek sell organic apples, veges and nuts from Estamore, their 8-hectare block bordering the Ruamahanga River. Roz has been saving her own garlic seed for a decade and harvests up to 4000 bulbs each year. She sells some through Commonsense Organics in Wellington but most goes to her sheep. Roz crushes her garlic with cider vinegar to make a general purpose drench.

At the Clevedon Farmers' Market, stallholder Stella Christoffersen, from Running Brook Seeds, sells gargantuan organic garlic, so a few years ago I hit her up for advice. Garlic loves muck, she told me. If you want bulbs as big as your fist, rather than piddly spheres the size of spring onions, the trick is to feed your soil first. Ahead of planting, Stella beefs up her garlic bed with lashings of cow manure and sheep pellets, then serves up liquid lunches of worm wee and seaweed throughout September and October, when the plants are swelling rapidly.

I put in 50 seed cloves today, at the far end of the asparagus bed behind the stables, and next month I'll plant 50 more. I also squeezed in a row of elephant garlic (*Allium ampeloprasum* var. *ampeloprasum*), though, botanically, that's actually a fat-bottomed leek.

GARLIC LOVES MUCK. THE TRICK IS TO FEED YOUR SOIL FIRST

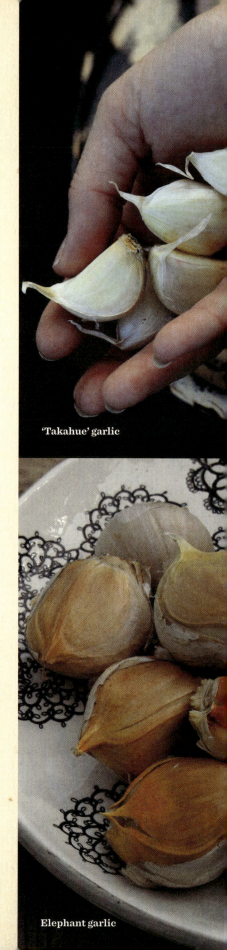

'Takahue' garlic

Elephant garlic

'Kakanui' garlic

JUNE 25: My garden is in a sorry state. The autumn fallen leaves that less than a month ago upholstered our gravel driveway in a technicoloured carpet have rotted into brown slurry. My vege patch is pitiful, though, as per usual, there's more 'Fordhook Giant' silverbeet than we can eat. Its deep green leaves are lush and glossy – even the snails aren't keen on eating it. Mum used to boil it till the stalks were as clear as window panes, but it's far nicer steamed and served with crispy bacon bits and sautéed onion, though most of my crop is destined for the chooks.

In front of the stables, the hop vines are bare and bitterly twisted. It's time to chop them down and mulch the crowns. At the far end of our lawn, dozens of sunflowers – so chipper in summer – are now skeletal shadows of their former selves. At least they'll provide carbon for our compost heap.

The wildflower border from our wedding is now bereft of blooms – and anything else for that matter. Only a desperate beneficial insect would seek board and lodgings here. But I'm not too fussed. Winter misery is the price you pay for spring glory in a cottage garden.

Flax

Hop vines

WINTER MISERY IS THE PRICE YOU PAY FOR SPRING GLORY IN A COTTAGE GARDEN

'Liberty' apples and 'Jelly King' crabapples

JUNE 27: How did new mothers cope before slow cookers were invented? What's not to love about lamb casseroles and lazy, bung-it-all-in-and-hope-for-the-best beef stews? I just wish someone would manufacture a slightly more compact model. I can't face the same meal more than three nights in a row and my husband's increasingly suspicious of my leftover slow-cooker-stew pies.

I've pinched Mum's pie maker – she won it in the cake decorating competition at the annual Paparimu Possum Hunt last month. Our farm hasn't been hunted in 15 years, but community spirit got the better of me so I entered a team. Jason, Dad and I spent a fruitless night firing bullets into our pine trees but failed to murder a single marsupial, though 1872 local possums (and 31 rabbits and two stoats) weren't quite so lucky.

IT SEEMS THAT POSSUMS HAVE SURPRISINGLY SOPHISTICATED PALATES

It seems that possums have surprisingly sophisticated palates. The winning team bagged 634 of the critters, courtesy of a 20-litre tub of strawberry jam. They smeared it over the fence posts along the edge of a bush block and, when their prey came out for a snack, they simply popped them off one by one. Why waste your jam though? I'd rather buy a Timms trap and bait it with star-anise-spiced scone dough or apples dusted in cinnamon.

Speaking of apples, I can't abide the gelatinous gloop that passes for apple purée in store-bought apple pies, so it's a good thing that our 'Liberty' trees were laden last season. I've still got half a dozen jars of apple sauce in the pantry.

You can never have too many apples, so I've just ordered five bare-root 'Peasgood Nonsuch' and five 'Bramley's Seedling' trees. 'Peasgood Nonsuch' has fruit the size of bowling balls, while 'Bramley's Seedling' is an English classic dating back to 1810 with large, round, red-cheeked fruit and firm, acidic flesh.

Bacon and egg pies

Slow-cooker-stew pies

JUNE 30: Love is blind. On our third date, Jason brought me a bunch of candy-pink camellias from a shrub halfway up his driveway. The gesture was so romantic that I didn't have the heart to tell him how much I loathe these blobby bushes.

In my city garden, I only grew two – the blood red, ruffled 'Takanini' and black red 'Night Rider' – but I'm coming around to camellias since moving to the country. They're so obliging, although our white camellias invariably bloom just in time for frosts to pulverise their petals.

Someone told me once that camellias should be artfully pruned to allow a sparrow to fly through their branches. If any bird tried to fly through the pink- and white-flowered camellia bushes (they were here when I came – I've no idea of their names) at the far end of our lawn, it'd get concussion.

Sasanqua camellias like 'Early Pearly' and 'Mine No Yuki' are the only ones deemed tasteful by contemporary garden designers, but I'd rather grow the old-fashioned formal japonicas like 'Desire' and 'EG Waterhouse'. Their flowers last surprisingly well in a vase and, in June, beggars can't be choosers: aside from a clump of mightily confused jonquils (the mild start to winter has fooled them into blooming two months early), I've nothing else to pick.

Camellias aren't my favourite, but they do cheer up a winter garden

Nyssa sylvatica

JULY 1: My neighbour Greg has hooked his weather station up to the internet. His data shows that it's not just wet (our rainfall so far this year is three times what it usually is), it's also weirdly warm. Lucas has a chest of drawers full of hand-knitted cardigans and caps from kindly *NZ Gardener* readers, but he's hardly needed them. After the warmest May on record, June followed suit and we haven't had a frost yet, though the nights are cool enough to stall our heat pump. I'm stockpiling pine cones to fire up the outdoor brazier that Jason cleverly welded for our wedding.

WE HAVEN'T HAD A FROST YET, THOUGH THE NIGHTS ARE COOL ENOUGH TO STALL OUR HEAT PUMP

JULY 4: I've heard about new dads who change careers, develop DIY obsessions and start stock market portfolios post-birth, but my man isn't so conventional. He's suddenly obsessed with making compost. Perhaps disposable nappy guilt is to blame.

I should never have told him that fallen leaves are such a valuable source of carbon for compost heaps. When Lucas naps, he bolts up the driveway with the quad bike and trailer to shovel loads of liquidambar sludge. I've never seen a man work so willingly – he's out there slashing down last summer's wildflowers and gathering up pulled weeds with his pitchfork.

The lawn, which hadn't been mown for six weeks, has now been trimmed to within an inch of its life, and all because I told him that grass clippings are rich in nitrogen. Shame he hasn't yet taken the hint about adding the contents of the vacuum cleaner bag to his heap though. Just imagine how spick and span our house would be.

JULY 6: I whipped down the road to the local tree nursery in Ramarama this morning. It was the first time I've been to a garden centre since Lucas was born. Retail fever got the better of me and I bought so many trees they have to deliver them by truck tomorrow.

I'm planning a citrus grove around the established 'Meyer' lemon tree in the top terraced bed below our house, so I bought a 'Seminole' tangelo (the best for juicing), 'Satsuma' and 'Clementine' mandarins, a pair of Tahitian limes, 'Villa Franca' and 'Lisbon' lemons, a kaffir lime, two grapefruit trees – 'Golden Special' and 'Cutler's Red' – and a super-sweet, easy-peel 'Lemonade'.

I also bought six 1.8m grafted ornamental 'Awanui' cherries and two 'Shimidsu Sakura' for their bountiful blossoms, plus three 'Goldmine' nectarines and a dozen *Nyssa sylvatica* for autumn colour in the swamp.

That'll teach Jason for letting me loose without the baby for an hour.

JULY 10: I haven't quite got to grips with motherhood yet. I'm lucky if I get out of my pyjamas before midday (truth be told, I'm lucky if I get out of them at all). It's like Groundhog Day, but instead of being beholden to the barometric whims of a rodent in a burrow, my every minute is betrothed to the bodily functions of a 5kg bundle of my own DNA.

I'm quite chuffed with our little lad, but cabin fever has kicked in. I fear I'm turning into one of those desperate housewives who pounce on their poor husbands the second they set foot in the door. My man can't even get his boots off before I launch into a detailed rundown of the day's events: how many burps, how many bowel motions, and Fifi's latest crazy craft project on *Good Morning*.

I'm not used to keeping myself company all day, so I've taken up cooking to kill time. Our freezer's fast filling up with soup.

My favourite flavours? Leek and potato, minestrone, Italian ribollita (it's the only reason, aside from its good looks in the garden, that I grow cavolo nero) and pea and smoked ham hock. Soup's so cheap and so satisfying. Even when my vege garden's at its most miserable, there's always enough for a pot of soup.

A few winters ago we set up a soup kitchen in the *NZ Gardener* office. I took in my slow cooker and every day a different staff member threw something into the pot. I made cauliflower soup; our designer Sarah made a Portuguese broth of chopped kale known as caldo verde; and our deputy editor Barb made red lentil and dried apricot soup (which, I confess, sounded dubious but was superb).

Our experiment came a little unstuck the day I made five litres of Jerusalem artichoke soup. One of our colleagues at *NZ House & Garden* magazine complained about the, shall we say, earthy aroma.

Cavolo nero

Barb's apricot and red lentil soup

In a large pot, gently fry 1 chopped onion, 1 cubed potato and a few smashed garlic cloves in a generous glug of olive oil. When soft, add 1 cup chopped dried apricots, 2 cups dried red lentils and at least 1 litre chicken stock (more if you prefer a thin soup). Season with cinnamon or ground cumin and simmer slowly until the lentils are tender. Blend for a smooth soup or leave chunky. Add a squeeze of lemon juice to each bowl and season to taste.

Minestrone soup

Jerusalem artichokes

I've been growing Jerusalem artichokes (*Helianthus tuberosus*) since 2007, when I started with half a dozen knobbly tubers from the City Farmers' Market in downtown Auckland. I'll never be without them again, though not entirely by choice. These perennial sunflowers grow like weeds. I now have, and this is a conservative estimate, about 2000 tubers.

Jerusalem artichokes have everything going for them. They're easy to grow, low in calories and an excellent alternative to starchy spuds. They're also diabetic-friendly, as they store their energy as the fructose polymer insulin, an indigestible form of carbohydrate that doesn't convert to sugar in our bloodstream. Unfortunately, all that undigested insulin also causes gas, hence their popular nickname, fartichokes.

Cooking Jerusalem artichokes with bay leaves, milk or caraway seeds can lessen their windy effects, as can waiting till after the first frosts to harvest them. Or you can just embrace the gas. (Researchers in Virginia are investigating the commercial potential of Jerusalem artichokes as biofuel. The tubers can yield 20 per cent ethanol after fermentation.)

Jerusalem artichoke soup

Scrub, peel and chop 500g Jerusalem artichokes, 1 onion, 2 'Agria' potatoes and 2 cloves garlic. Place in a soup pot with 2–3 tablespoons olive oil and sauté, shaking occasionally, for 5 minutes. Add 4 cups chicken stock and your choice of chopped fresh herbs, and simmer until the vegetables are soft. Take off the heat and purée with a stick blender until smooth. Stir in 1 cup cream or a pottle of crème fraîche, season to taste and garnish with chopped chives to serve. If you're afraid of the social consequences, swap the artichokes for a similar quantity of cauliflower or celeriac.

JULY 14: We've had a week of torrential rain. The spouting on the front of the stables collapsed and flooded my rose garden, there's more mud than grass in the paddocks and, to make matters worse, I left my gumboots out on the deck overnight and they filled up with water.

There are slim pickings in my vege patch too – scrawny leeks, stringy celery, mint, yams, rhubarb, lemons, 'Precoce Romanesco' broccoli, chives, spring onions . . . but nowt else.

On the telly tonight they're debating food prices. Tomatoes are fetching $15.98 a kg and capsicums are $3.99 each. Yet the fruit and vege store in Drury has Southland swedes for $1.50 – and they're the size of bowling balls. Does no one eat seasonally anymore?

(I'd eat my own swedes, but so far they've progressed only to ping-pong-ball status.

THERE ARE SLIM PICKINGS IN MY VEGE PATCH

They'd better be ready by the time Lucas cuts his first tooth.)

JULY 16: Winter smells so different in the sticks. There's the petrolhead perfume of passing stock trucks, the lanolin scent of steaming sheep, the whiff of a working man's wet socks, the gut-wrenching stench of silage and the sweet breath of cattle chewing molasses-soaked hay. Only our cats smell of summer. They're spending their days holed up in the hay barn.

Feeding out hay was my least favourite job as a kid. I always felt sorry for our wet, wretched herd. Grass was strictly rationed in the weeks before calving – our cows got a quarter of a paddock each day, with a tenth of a bale each for breakfast.

Our beef cattle don't do it half as hard as a dairy herd. Hay's a treat here.

Gypsy and Mr Puppy-Doo-Hawg
don't mind the mud

JULY 17: I am not a morning person. I never have been. As a child I'd crawl out of bed at the last possible moment and was always cutting it fine to catch the school bus. (I can't help but admire my niece Jaime's cunning. This week, in a time-saving stroke of pure genius, she put her school uniform on under her pyjamas. She would have got away with it too, had my sister not gone in to wish her goodnight only to spot her school shirt collar poking out of the blankets.)

I am not a morning person, but since Lucas was born, I've seen in the dawn more often than not. Fog creeps in under the cover of darkness, so that when the sun rises all I can see are the silhouetted trees around our lawn and the seemingly dismembered tips of the Hunua Ranges on the horizon.

WHEN THE SUN RISES ALL I CAN SEE ARE THE SILHOUETTED TREES AROUND OUR LAWN

Jason no longer needs to set his alarm clock. If it's a misty morning, as it almost always is, I bellow up the stairs, 'It's foggy on Foggydale Farm!'

By the time it's light enough to take a decent photo, the fog lifts. It must be for my eyes only. And Lucas's, too, though to be quite honest at that time of the day he's rather more interested in what's up my shirt than what's out the window.

JULY 20: I'd only known Jason for two weeks when I suggested he should plant an orchard. It's lucky he was amenable to the idea, because I'd already ordered him 100 bare-root trees – 40 almonds, 25 apples, 20 pears, five 'Jelly King' crabapples (for cider), five sour cherries (for cherry pie) and five 'Damson' plums (for jam).

My mates, not to mention my parents, thought I was mad at the time but I'm glad I jumped the gun and got on with it. Two years down the track, our pantry is already loaded with jars of 'Damson' plum jam and stewed apples, though we're yet to see a cherry (I'm sure the birds enjoyed them) or pear. As for the almonds, our entire crop numbered 13 this year, after a savage string of frosts hammered the delicate pale pink spring blossoms last winter. Almonds live dangerously – they're the first fruit tree to flower here.

In 2010 I added two 'Blackboy' peaches, two 'Flatto' peaches, two hybrid 'Healey's Peacherines', a 'Gobstopper' plum and a purple mulberry tree to the mix.

And this year? I've ordered 10 more heirloom 'Blackboy' peaches (I've been told they'll do well here) and 10 'Seckel' pears to espalier, plus five of each of the following: 'Tomcot' apricots (a new variety with large, peach-sized, freestone fruit on a compact tree); 'Golden Queen' peaches (a must-have for bottling); 'Queen Giant' nectarines; 'Elephant Heart' and 'Santa Rosa' plums; 'Smyrna' quinces (large, aromatic fruit and attractive foliage); and 'Spring Satin' plumcots (a cross between a plum and an apricot, with early season crops of sweet, golden-fleshed, reddish black-skinned fruit). Oh, and a pair of sassy, purple-leafed 'Mabel' nectarines, just because they looked gorgeous in the catalogue. 'Mabel' has been bred from a chance seedling that popped up in a Waikato garden.

It's too frosty here to grow tamarillos – I'm content to swipe them off my sister's tree – but I definitely need a red cherry guava. There's a marvellous old tree in my city garden that's laden every winter; I must pop past to pinch the fruit. If you don't mind their many pips, cherry guavas add a tantalising tang to winter crumbles. I've given up making guava jelly though. Mine never sets.

Frosted almond blossom

Red cherry guavas

'Ted's Red' tamarillos

Brown shavers are the best layers

JULY 22: When they're all on the lay, our seven brown shaver hens pump out 49 eggs a week. We eat sponge cake and proper custard, bacon and egg pies, fresh fettuccine and crème brûlée in a bid to boil, poach, scramble and soufflé our way through dozens of pavlova-perfect whites and sunshine-yellow yolks. Jason can knock back nine eggs at a time in an omelette and Mr Puppy Doo-Hawg's record is two dozen (I accidentally left the egg bucket on the deck one night), but our fridge is always full of eggs.

Except in winter. Last week we collected eight eggs; this week, a frugal four. It really doesn't bode well for next week.

In the days before fridges, my grandmothers preserved surplus eggs for winter with Ovaline (a paste, similar to Vaseline, which was smeared over the porous shells to make them airtight) or water glass (sodium silicate). Marketed as Norton's Egg Preserver, water glass was diluted nine parts to one – a shilling tin was enough to preserve 36 dozen eggs – in a four-gallon kerosene tin.

Water glass was vile, slimy stuff to sink your hand into, Grandma recalls. When cracked, the yolks invariably separated and the flavour was a bit off, but preserved eggs were perfectly good for baking.

Our chooks are free-range, to a point. They share an old horse pen with our plum and cherry trees, and five dwarf 'Initial' apples. 'Initial' is a modern variety that's disease resistant, but not beak-proof. When the branches are laden, they droop to hen height.

Every so often I take pity on our birds and let them out to forage for a day, but they invariably take advantage of the situation by demolishing my brassicas or raiding my rhubarb bed.

Rhubarb leaves, as any gardener knows, are poisonous. Thrifty green thumbs boil up the toxic foliage in a pot of water, strain it off and add a generous squirt of dishwashing detergent to make a natural pesticide spray for nix. (Just don't re-use the pot in your kitchen.)

Rhubarb insecticide kills aphids and caterpillars, but not, it seems, chooks. Mine can, and do, strip every centimetre of foliage off the stalks without any ill effects.

I'd like to raise my own meat birds, though our attempts so far haven't been entirely successful. Of the four chicks we've hatched to date, two grew into feral roosters, one was a little white hen . . . and the other came to an untimely end before his gender could be determined.

There was great excitement when our first chick hatched on Christmas Day. We promptly christened it JC (Jesus Chicken – no offence intended). It's a Hallinan family tradition. If you look through our summer photo album from 1995, you'll spot JC (Jesus Calf) lurking inside our house. The Christmas product of a somewhat less than immaculate conception – the neighbour's Hereford bull jumped the fence and got one of Dad's empty cows up the duff out of season – Jesus Calf was a Good Samaritan. He gave his life for those less fortunate. Dad bequeathed him to the IHC's donate-a-calf fundraising scheme and off he went to the works, none the wiser.

Jesus Chicken didn't see death coming either – he was snatched by a hawk – and his father, our pedigree silver-laced Wyandotte rooster Frederico, met his maker soon after, prematurely ending our meat bird breeding programme.

Jason and his mate Boogie accidentally shot Frederico while aiming at one of his delinquent sons. We roasted the evidence with honeyed carrots and golden 'Beauregard' kumara, and served up our remaining cockerels as coq au vin.

> ### *Coq au vin*
> Too many roosters?
> Chop up a whole cockerel and marinate the pieces overnight in a bottle of good Burgundy or pinot noir, then pop into a slow cooker with a splash of olive oil, 20 pickling onions, 6 garlic cloves, a packet of manuka smoked bacon, 1 cup button mushrooms, bay leaves, fresh thyme and parsley. Cook on low all day.

Crème brûlée

Fresh pasta

In a bid to motivate our men to cook more often, my sister and I bought our blokes pasta machines for Christmas. When you have laying chooks, fresh pasta is cheap – and a cinch to make. The basic recipe is 1 egg per 100g flour (preferably Italian 00-grade), plus a generous pinch of sea salt. Make a well in the flour and break the eggs into it, mix into a small ball of dough, knead for five minutes, then roll through a pasta machine. Hang the pasta on a drying rack once it's cut.

Lasagne sheets, spaghetti and fettuccine are our staples, while ravioli is for special occasions. I stuff these pasta parcels with Buffalo ricotta from the Clevedon Farmers' Market, lemon zest, grated Parmesan and finely chopped fresh herbs. In summer, I use the same filling to stuff zucchini blossoms which I shallow fry in tempura batter.

Crème brûlée

Give a man dessert and he'll eat for a day . . . but give him a chef's professional blow torch and he'll make you crème brûlée. This baked custard is Jason's signature dessert (he's pretty good at making pavlova with the leftover egg whites too).

Preheat oven to 150°C. In a small pot, heat 2 cups cream and a vanilla pod, split in half with the seeds scraped into the cream, until it just boils. While the cream is heating, beat 4 large egg yolks with ½ cup sugar and a pinch of salt. Slowly pour the hot cream into the egg mixture, whisking constantly (don't pour it all at once or you'll end up with sweet scrambled eggs). Strain through a sieve to remove any lumps, then divide into six small ramekins. Place ramekins in a roasting dish and add enough boiling water to come halfway up the sides. Bake for 25–30 minutes, until the custard is jiggly. When cool, pop in the fridge. When ready to serve, sprinkle with 1–2 teaspoons caster sugar and blast, gently, with a blow torch until the sugar melts and caramelises into a hard shell.

WHEN THEY'RE ALL ON THE LAY, OUR SEVEN BROWN SHAVER HENS PUMP OUT 49 EGGS A WEEK

Pavlova

Preheat oven to 150°C (or pop in a pav when you take out your crème brûlées). In a large clean bowl, beat 4 egg whites until stiff. Add 50ml water and beat again. Gradually add 1¼ cups caster sugar and beat until glossy, then fold in 1 tablespoon cornflour, 1 teaspoon vanilla extract and 1 teaspoon white vinegar. Line an oven tray with baking paper, spread pavlova mixture into a round shape and bake for 45 minutes. Turn off oven and, if you're worried about your pavlova collapsing, don't open the door until it's cool.

Scotch eggs

My Chinese Silkie hen, Onion, lays dinky white eggs about half the size of a size 6 egg, which means they lean lopsidedly in every egg cup I own. On the plus side, they're easy to encase in sausage meat for classic, but rather cute, Scotch eggs.

Hardboil half a dozen Chinese Silkie eggs (or 4 standard eggs). Peel and set aside. Combine 400g sausage meat, ½ onion, finely diced, a handful of chopped fresh parsley, salt, pepper and a squeeze of tomato sauce in a bowl and mix well. Divide into equal portions and mould around each egg. Roll in breadcrumbs then shallow fry in hot oil for 8–10 minutes until outsides are golden and meat is cooked through. Cut in half to serve.

JULY 23 : It's so cold at night that my ginger beer bug doesn't so much bubble constantly as let out the occasional burp. It has been chugging along in an Agee jar on the kitchen windowsill since May, so it's probably due for retirement, but I'm determined to keep it going for longer than the sourdough starter I accidentally starved at the back of our fridge. I have a love-hate relationship with yeast.

When I was a kid, we knew our ginger beer was ready to drink when the bottles started exploding under the kitchen bench – though I prefer to recycle plastic soft drink bottles these days. It helps salve my conscience about all those disposable nappies that Lucas is getting through.

Ginger beer

Ginger beer

It only takes a week to grow a ginger beer bug (I don't know why it's called a bug; in Mum's day it was called a plant). Start with 2 tablespoons dried active yeast, 1 teaspoon sugar, 1 teaspoon ground ginger and 1 cup water. Mix together in a jar, cover with a piece of muslin held in place with a rubber band, and store somewhere warm overnight.

The next day, and every day after that, feed your bug with 1 teaspoon sugar and 1 teaspoon ginger. After a week, you're ready to bottle your first batch of fizz.

Dissolve 2 cups sugar in 1 litre boiling water, add the juice of 2–3 lemons and top up to 5 litres with cold water. Add the liquid strained off the top of the bug, stir well, and bottle. Then give your bug a pat on the back, a fresh glass of water and start feeding it all over again for your next batch.

Ginger beer's easy to make, and versatile too. If I'm making Christmas trifle for kids, I'll soak the sponge in ginger beer instead of booze.

Paul Jobin's ginger corned beef

When I heard chef Paul Jobin giving out his recipe for corned beef in ginger beer on the radio recently, I stopped my car and wrote it down. When you've home-killed a beast, there's always an interminable supply of corned silverside to get through.

Method: Slice 1 onion, a knob of ginger, 1 orange, 1 lemon and 1 fresh chilli. Place in a large pot with 1 corned silverside, 1 bay leaf, 4 sprigs thyme, 2 bottles ginger beer and enough extra water to cover the beef. Bring to the boil and simmer for 90 minutes. Cool in the stock.

JULY 24: I'm not a very good matchmaker. In May, we introduced my mother-in-law's long-in-the-tooth ram, Rambo, to our 12 ewes. He doesn't look like he's up to the job, but Maureen assures me he's a lascivious Lothario when nobody's watching.

We've actually got 13 ewes but my nephew Sam's first pet lamb, Harold, thinks she's a cow. Sam was going through a Thomas the Tank Engine phase when he named her after Harold the Helicopter. The masculine moniker stuck and Harold is now mutton dressed as ram.

Harold was destined to be mutton dressed in a hangi basket after my brother-in-law Alan booked her in for a one-way trip to the butcher. But Dad intervened, negotiated a stay of execution, and let her run with his heifers on their lifestyle block. Harold, however, doesn't know the meaning of the word run. All she does is eat. In fact she ate so much that, two years later, she was too fat to run up the ramp into Dad's mate Neal's shearing shed. It took three blokes – Dad, Neal and Alan – to manhandle her into position.

Dad swore he'd never shear Harold again, so he put her on his trailer and sent her to a fat farm. Our farm. We put her in with our sheep but it was too late; she refused to integrate. She took up a possie under one of the plane trees by the cattle yards and spent a lonely week wailing over the fence at our cows, until we ceded and opened the gate.

Harold now runs, or more accurately waddles, with our steers. She isn't the slightest bit interested in Rambo, and the feeling's mutual.

JULY 25: They're predicting a sprinkling of snow on the Hunua Ranges tonight. I'll believe it when I see it.

Harold

JULY 26: The snow was a no-show but we woke this morning to iced fence posts, frozen puddles and a lawn that crunches like a bowl of rice bubbles underfoot. I was horrified to find my metre-high ornamental tobacco plants (*Nicotiana mutabilis*) flattened by the frost, their flannelette foliage crumpled and slumped, but by midday they'd perked back up. *Nicotiana mutabilis* is one of my favourite perennials, with chameleon bells of pink, white and rose, so I'm pleased that it's hardier than it looks.

We only get a few sub-zero nights on our farm each year. They powder-coat the paddocks white, dust our unshorn sheep with shaved ice and cause all the camellia flowers

Ice-crystallised clover

A SHORT, SHARP COLD SNAP ISN'T ALL BAD

to drop to the ground like clumps of soiled tissue. But this year I couldn't care less about the frost-bitten rhodo. I'm content to wait winter out, with the home fires burning (well, the heat pump on high), happily distracted by a baby who has just cracked his first smile … and a bowl of Nelson-grown hard-shelled almonds to crack.

A short, sharp cold snap isn't all bad anyway. Freezing temperatures will sweeten the flavour of my baby parsnips, swedes and yams, as these hardy root crops convert carbohydrates to sugar to produce a natural sort of antifreeze. Brussels sprouts and kale – especially the traditional European curly-headed types like 'Squire' – also taste better after a hard frost. Plus nippy nights send pests packing and an icy spell shatters clods of compacted clay soil more effectively than any husband with a rotary hoe. Jack Frost is cruel to citrus trees though. For the past two years, I've been protecting our lemon tree, and the grafted passionfruit vine growing along the front of the stables, with an organic wax spray called Liquid Frost Cloth. If only I'd got around to spraying my new citrus grove …

Hard-shelled 'Monovale' almonds

Night Rider

AUGUST 5: I'm living dangerously. I've planted my first row of 'Jersey Benne' spuds. It's far too early but I can't wait any longer. There's a slim chance the worst frosts will have passed by the time their tender leafy tops emerge from the soil.

I'm converting the raised rock-walled bed around the cherry blossom tree by our front door into a new vege patch, with all my crops in neat rows. I laid down a rake to mark the first trenches, then filled them with 'Cos' lettuces, two rows of garlic, onions, arugula (perennial rocket), celery and 'Red Glow' calendulas.

I'm not sure how successful it will be, given that I've already had to chase the dogs out of there twice today, and the cats seem to think it's a giant litter box, conveniently located two steps and a jump from the cat flap.

AUGUST 6: Our first daffodil! That first hint of spring went straight to my head. While Lucas was having his morning nap, I snuck outside with the baby monitor in my back pocket and put in another three rows of 'Jersey Benne' spuds. My aim is to capture the Clevedon Farmers' Market with them come Christmas.

AUGUST 11: It might be wise for my husband to confiscate my credit card. Since moving down the line, I've developed such an addiction to online shopping that our postie, Bernie, is on first-name terms with our dogs. 'Hello, Gypsy darling,' she coos to our brindle Beagle-Bitzer as she piles parcels on our deck.

This week's deliveries include a clutch of carrot seeds, lip balm from The Herb Farm and a stretchy Spandex nursing top that promised to be 'forgiving, yet flattering, and effortlessly chic'. And it is, if you ignore the milk stains down the front.

I'VE DEVELOPED AN ADDICTION TO ONLINE SHOPPING

The international craft website Etsy.com and TradeMe's antiques and collectables category account for the lion's share of my purchases. I can't resist old crystal comports, silver spoons, green art glass and retro kitchenware. Life's too short to sift flour, but not to bid for vintage flour sifters, fruit corers, potato ricers, herb cutters and other labour-saving gizmos from my grandmothers' era. My Spong bean slicer is my favourite bit of kit, though it's good for nothing. It chokes on 'Scarlet Runner' strings like a lawnmower with a mouthful of fallen cordyline leaves.

I've never bought anything alive from TradeMe before, but this morning I snapped up an orphaned chocolate-coloured ram lamb from a farmer in Bombay. (I saved Bernie a trip and picked him up myself.)

Dad thinks I'm mad to pay $90 for a pet lamb, but we need a new ram. If Rambo has successfully serviced our ewes this season, it won't do to let him loose on his daughters next year.

AUGUST 12: When Mum got married, she wasn't much of a cook. She didn't need to be. She had her mum's battered copy of the original Women's Division of the Federated Farmers' Cookbook, packed with time-honoured recipes and jaunty sayings for chipper country housewives.

I'm working my way through Chapter 16, 'Puddings – Baked', which begins, 'When nights are cold and days are short, And the family's in from work or sport, They'll love the Mum whose oven's got, A good baked pudding, steaming hot.'

I'm partial to treacle steamed puddings, but my favourite pud from the past is a simple fruit sponge. It was Mum's standby on winter nights when she hadn't time to make apple dumplings or lemon meringue pie. She'd upend a litre jar of bottled 'Black Doris' plums into a roasting dish, heat the fruit till it was piping hot, then spoon over sponge batter and bake it while we ate our dinner.

A fruit sponge should be golden and fluffy on top, slightly soggy and stained purple with plum juice (or even better, bottled 'Blackboy' peaches) below. Hypersensitive food safety officials would have conniptions these days, but our puddings were served with cream as thick as custard, scraped straight off the top of the 10-litre milk pail.

I don't have any bottled plums this winter – our tree had only six fruit last summer – but we do have plenty of poached pears. In my city garden, there's an old pear tree – possibly 'Williams' Bon Chrétien' or 'Packham's Triumph' – that's as tall as the house. Its arthritic limbs are encrusted with lichen, but every year it produces a bumper crop of plump, freckled pears. I picked its last crop green in mid-March (if left to ripen fully on the tree, pears invariably rot from the inside out) and lugged them home to the farm in bulging black plastic rubbish bags.

Mum and I spent a pleasant autumn afternoon peeling, coring, slicing and bottling pears, some in sugar syrup with a split vanilla pod, the others poached in pinot noir with cinnamon, whole cloves, brown sugar and star anise. We filled two dozen jars, enough for a pear pudding every week until spring.

Mum's fruit sponge pudding

Preheat oven to 190°C. Grease a baking dish and empty a 1 litre jar of bottled fruit into it. Pop into the oven while you make the sponge topping. In a large bowl, cream 125g butter, 1 teaspoon vanilla and ½ cup sugar. Add 2 eggs, one at a time, beating after each addition, then fold in 1 cup flour, 2 teaspoons baking powder and ½ cup milk. Spoon batter over hot fruit and bake for 30–40 minutes, until the sponge is golden and springy on top. Serve hot with ice cream or custard.

My fave pear for bottling is 'Doyenne du Comice' – I must plant a tree of my own

AUGUST 13: If I hadn't already married my husband, I'd propose to him now, but only if his mother Maureen was part of the deal. She's a godsend. Today she kept Lucas entertained indoors (and cleaned the bathroom, dusted the glassware, vacuumed the floor and got to the bottom of the washing basket) while Jason and I got stuck into our new vege patch.

We earthed in four more bags of 'Jersey Benne' and two bags of 'Purple Heart' seed potatoes, 50 cloves of garlic and two rows of pink dahlia tubers, including my favourite from my wedding bouquet, 'Ruthie G'.

We also transplanted two trays of Dutch purple pea seedlings ('just like Grandpa used to grow') and 'Dwarf Massey' peas; two punnets of broccoflowers and 'Savoy' cabbages; three punnets of fragrant purple stock; four punnets of 'Artist's Glory' Iceland poppies and four punnets of 'Snowlands' chrysanthemums.

I didn't get as much done as I'd have liked, as there are still four trays of Russell lupins, a tray of beetroot, a tray of rocket and half a tray of swedes – can a girl grow too many swedes? I already have two rows in the garden – in the plastic propagating house on our deck.

AUGUST 14: When I moved to the country, I vowed not to create a garden so large I couldn't take care of it all. It's one of the pitfalls when you can push the boundaries whenever you want, simply by shifting the fences out.

My aim last summer was to grow annuals en masse – sunflowers, wildflowers, white cosmos, petunias, zinnias – for a snazzy display in our wedding photos. I hadn't planned any further ahead than mid-February. But six months down the track, it's impossible to ignore the obvious flaw in that plan. Everything's dead.

Although my plan this year is to plant annuals en masse again, they'll mainly be edible varieties

MAGNOLIA BRANCHES CREATE INSTANT IKEBANA IN GLAZED JUGS

to sell at the Clevedon Farmers' Market, and I'm putting in perennials and shrubs around the periphery. Jason hates hydrangeas, so I'm hoping he won't recognise the oak-leaf species, *Hydrangea quercifolia* 'Snowflake', that I've planted behind the purple rhododendron on the far side of the lawn.

To keep the bluebells company under the liquidambars, I've ordered 50 hellebores (*Helleborus orientalis*) with shy freckled faces in cream, lime and burgundy, plus penstemons, gauras, dianthus, echinaceas and a dozen *Saxifraga* 'Star Blush' for the beds at the end of the lawn.

Saxifraga 'Star Blush' is a rockery plant that produces a tight cushion of fleshy foliage rather like native scleranthus, but topped with rosy pink flowers in spring. Inspired by Beth Chatto's famous gravel garden in Essex, I once slotted it into the pea-gravel paths in my city garden. I thought it would look cute – like something out of an Enid Blyton storybook – and it did . . . until I opened my garden to the public. My subtle plant placement went over my visitors' heads and under their feet. The saxifrages were all stomped on.

I'll never tire of perennials but I am wary of shrubs. In my experience, most have a five-year best-by date, after which they develop a middle-aged shabbiness that can't be overcome with a nip-and-tuck pruning policy. However, I'll forgive *Philadelphus* 'Frosty Morn' and 'Virginal' – I've ordered five of each – for their scruffy appearance because their spring fragrance is so divine, and no garden would be complete without a daphne bush or three. Mine are blooming now beside the pink magnolias at the far end of the lawn. I pick branches of both, displaying the daphne in bud vases in the bathroom, while the magnolia branches create instant ikebana in glazed jugs on the kitchen bench.

Daphne odora

Magnolia

Saxifraga 'Star Blush'

Helleborus orientalis

Peas will germinate even in frosty soil

Sunflower

Rhododendron

AUGUST 15: It's snowing! Proper snow! Not slushy hail or sleety rain, but bona fide six-sided ice crystals swirling out of the clouds and settling on the dogs' backs.

I do hope it doesn't turn out to be a once-in-a-lifetime experience. I was so busy trying to film the flakes with my video camera without dropping Lucas that I failed to take a decent digital photo.

AUGUST 19: Red skies at night aren't just a shepherd's delight. Our power company's shareholders must be beside themselves with joy. We've had three hard frosts in a row this week, and possibly four. I can't say for sure, because Lucas slept past sunrise for the first time, giving the grass time to thaw.

I've never seen icicles clinging to the bare branches of my fruit trees before.

AUGUST 20: My snowdrops (*Galanthus nivalis*) and jonquils are flowering. It's a miracle, given that I only got the bulbs into the ground six weeks ago (and when I say 'I', I really mean my husband's cousin's wife Nicola, who has been helping me catch up on the gardening chores I missed in the weeks before, and after, Lucas was born). I can't really skite about those snowdrops though. They're the saddest wee things you've ever seen, with two chive-sized leaves and a tiny bell atop a 10-cm stalk.

AUGUST 21: The garden is starting to take shape. This weekend we planted two more rows of dahlias, two bags of 'Cliff's Kidney' seed potatoes, some Oriental poppies, 'Strawberry Parfait' dianthus and 'Bright Lights' silverbeet.

I also sowed 'Empress of India' nasturtiums between the silverbeet, Chinese 'Kai Laan' and purple kohlrabi beside my giant red mustard and a row of 'Onward' climbing peas along the fence.

Jonquils

Snowdrops

'Erlicheer'

I DON'T PLAN. I JUST PLANT

AUGUST 28: It really doesn't pay to marry a man with a mind of his own. Jason and I have been butting heads over the finer points of French formal garden design.

My childhood desire for a pony long forgotten, I've decided to convert the unused 56m by 22m equestrian arena below our house into a geometrical parterre garden enclosed by clipped hornbeam hedges, with a la-di-dah lawn and a fancy-pants potager. My darling husband had it earmarked for a go-kart track, but I soon quashed that idea.

Jason has many attractive assets, not least of which are his 20-tonne Hyundai, 12-tonne Hitachi, 10-tonne Hitachi, 4.5-tonne and 3-tonne Airman diggers (that last one dug all the holes for our orchard in an afternoon).

A man with land is a mighty fine catch, but a chap with earth-moving equipment is even better . . . except my husband's refusing to start digging until I've drawn a design plan. Not just in my head, or welded to my heart, but on paper.

I don't plan. I just plant. Even though I know all the design rules – plant five of this, and seven of that (odd numbers, apparently, are more aesthetically pleasing) – I ignore them.

Jason also expects me to stick to a planting plan. This could prove problematic. Whereas he likes to dig a hole, and then procure a plant to put in it, I am a shocking impulse buyer. On my most recent visit to the local garden centre, I went to buy rhubarb and came home with six punnets of love-in-the-mist, three sensationally citrus-scented Mexican marigolds (*Tagetes lemmonii*), a packet of 'Patricia Ann' sweet pea seeds and half a dozen 'Strawberry Mousse' brachyscome daisies. And no rhubarb.

In a bid to allay his fears that I'm making it all up as I go, and in the spirit of compromise, I waited until he went off on a boys' trip to the Bledisloe Cup this morning, then headed down the terraced hill with a can of blue spray paint and a long tape measure.

Maureen held Lucas while I marked out my new formal garden. It has 15 square beds at one end, to be mirrored by a 15-tree phalanx of red horse chestnut trees (*Aesculus* x *carnea*) at the other. The gravel paths will be wide enough for the quad bike and, in the middle, there's a scalloped lawn with embroidered parterres on the corners. I rather fancy a Victorian glasshouse too, or an ornate band rotunda like the one at Auckland Zoo, though it might pay to keep those plans to myself for now.

AUGUST 30: My new citrus trees have turned a sickly shade of yellow and are shedding their leaves. Eight hard frosts and a sprinkle of snow have proved too much for their tender, glasshouse-raised constitutions. I hope they don't die.

Our existing 'Meyer' lemon, at least, is laden with fruit and I can buy sweet mandarins from a roadside stall near Ramarama for $3 a kg. I craved mandarins when I was pregnant but they gave me chronic heartburn, so now I'm making up for lost time.

In frost-free climates it's possible to pick mandarins almost year round, starting with the early, easy-peel varieties 'Miho', 'Aoshima' and seedless 'Satsuma' in autumn, followed by 'Clementine' and 'Corsica No 2' in winter, 'Burgess Scarlet' in spring and 'Encore' in summer.

As much as I love mandarins, the citrus I am most nostalgic for is grapefruit. On our farm in Onewhero there was a prolific old grapefruit tree – a hunchbacked brute with borer-infested limbs lurching in every direction – in the middle of the back lawn.

We ate grapefruit for breakfast every day in winter – sliced in half, sprinkled with brown sugar and zapped in the microwave for 30 seconds – and possums stole their fair share too, but most of the fruit ended up rotting on the lawn.

Pulverising grapefruit made midwinter lawn mowing almost bearable. The blades clogged, the catcher choked and the wheels invariably got stuck in sodden ruts, but all that was forgiven with the first aromatic explosion underfoot. No scented candle or sauvignon blanc smells half as good or grassy to me as a fermenting grapefruit gutted by a mower.

My grandmother was probably glad to see the back of that tree when my parents took over the farm. Before she left, she taught Mum how to make marmalade – it's the first handwritten recipe in my mother's leather-bound book. I've just made five jars using fruit from Mum and Dad's mate Kay's garden in Clevedon.

Truth be told, I'd rather spread lemon curd on pancakes than eat marmalade on toast, but our chooks have gone off the lay and I resent buying eggs. Plus our lemons look a bit scabby this season – they've got citrus verrucosis, a fungal disease that doesn't affect the flavour or juiciness of the flesh, but does make zesting the skins somewhat tricky.

Mum's marmalade

Thinly slice 500g citrus fruit (take your pick from oranges, grapefruit and lemons) and soak overnight in 1.5 litres water. The next day, pour fruit and water into a large pot and bring slowly to the boil. Simmer, covered, for one hour until the fruit is tender. Add 1.5kg warmed sugar and boil hard for 30–40 minutes, uncovered. Pour into jars and seal.

Lemon curd

'Meyer' lemons are the most cold-hardy but these hybrids lack the acidity of true lemons, such as 'Lisbon', 'Yen Ben' or 'Villa Franca', so they can't be used to make limoncello liqueur (the one time I tried, I ended up with a bottle of lemon-flavoured slime). They're fine for making lemon curd though.

Method: Finely grate the zest of 4 large lemons and squeeze and strain the juice. Place in a small bowl over a pot of boiling water with 200g butter and 2 cups sugar. When the butter has melted and the sugar has dissolved, add 4 beaten eggs and whisk constantly until the curd thickens. Store in the fridge.

'Clementine' mandarins

'Golden Special' grapefruit

'Meyer' lemons

Limoncello

You name it, I've probably tried to infuse it in vodka, brandy or gin. I make my own zesty limoncello in winter, green walnut liqueur in spring, 'Damson' gin in summer and quince vodka in autumn. The basic method is the same. Take fruit, drown in alcohol, store in a dark cupboard for six months, strain, sweeten with sugar and imbibe.

Method: To make limoncello, carefully peel the zest off a dozen large lemons, avoiding the bitter pith. Pack the peels into a glass jar and top with a bottle of cheap vodka. Leave to infuse for at least a month, then strain and sweeten to taste with a heavy sugar syrup (bring 2 cups sugar and 1 cup water to the boil, simmer until sugar has dissolved, then cool).

OUR 'MEYER' LEMON IS RARELY WITHOUT FRUIT – OR BLOSSOMS

WAIT TILL THE SOIL STEAMS IN THE EARLY MORNING SUN, SHE SAYS

AUGUST 31: After a season of sleepless nights, frosty mornings and freakish snow, spring is almost here. The first almond blossoms are out and the cherries can't be far behind.

Today I planted calendulas (their orange petals give loaves of bread a pumpkin glow), a punnet of 'Perpetual Green' silverbeet (it's a spinach lookalike) and a rainbow of cauliflowers: white 'Phenomenal Early', Fanta-coloured 'Orange Bouquet' and purple-pink 'Violet Sicilian'.

I've sown 'Dwarf Early Green' and rare (in New Zealand at least) crimson-flowered broad beans; a packet of white-seeded peans (a Dalmatian heirloom drying bean with round, white, pea-like seeds) and a row of 'Bull's Blood' beetroot. I haven't sown any broccoli. It's one of Jason's favourite vegetables but I think it's ghastly, gritty stuff. I won't grow it.

I'm itching to sow carrots too – I'm determined to break my jinx by sowing every variety you can buy – but Stella from Running Brook Seeds advises caution. Wait till the soil steams in the early morning sun, she says. Only then can you be sure that spring has sprung.

Pea and purple stock seedlings

SPRING

As the soil temperature starts
to rise, so do my spirits.
Spring is the season of hope.

Blue anemones

Red cabbage

Daffodils

'Savoy' cabbage

'Giant Red' mustard

Globe artichoke

ALL WINTER, I WAIT FOR SPRING TO ARRIVE. I flip the pages on the calendar with such excitement and anticipation. And what happens next? Nothing . . . just more rain, more mud, more frosts, more bellowing bovines.

SEPTEMBER 1: Despite daily patrols of my asparagus plot, there's not a spear to be seen and, if it weren't for the daffodils and early stone-fruit blossoms, it would still look like midwinter on our farm.

The leaves won't return to the trees for at least another month, but there's hope, or at least hops, on the horizon. The buds on the hop vines (*Humulus lupulus*) I brought home from Nelson have sprouted their first Velcro tendrils. Apparently you can eat the young tips like spring asparagus, though they don't look particularly appetising to me.

SEPTEMBER 3: My paternal grandfather, Percy, had a soft spot for gladioli. Grandma reckons that, had he only one bob left to his name, he'd have spent it on gladioli. They were his favourite flower; he put in a whole bed of them on the farm in Huntly.

Jason's grandfather, Fred, grew gladioli too. He remembers helping to pick the long stems – their Latin name *gladiolus* translates as 'little sword' – to give to visitors. I originally ordered green gladdies for the blokes' buttonholes at our wedding, but the grower let us down and they ended up with lime lisianthus instead.

In the Victorian language of flowers, gladioli symbolise sincerity, generosity and strength of character. I sincerely hope they're generous and strong in my garden, because I've just ordered 285 corms to plant – 20 each of striped red and white 'Zizanie', pink-throated 'Flevo Dancer' and dusky dark purple 'Flevo Waris' from Garden Post, and 25 each of white 'Divinity'; pale green 'Hint o' Mint', 'Dave's Memory', 'Green Isle' and 'Limerick'; ruffled apricot 'Double Contessa'; 'Wine and Roses'; 'Phantom'; and 'Bewitched' from NZ Bulbs online.

I didn't stop at gladioli, either. I ordered five 'Festival Pink' gypsophila, 40 lily bulbs and a box of newspaper-wrapped seedlings from Awapuni Nurseries: white honesty, red stock, 'Buttercrunch' lettuce, 'Pearl Drop' onions and an acid-green euphorbia lookalike called *Bupleurum* 'Griffithii'.

SEPTEMBER 4: We're not eating much out of our vegetable garden, because there's not much in it – aside from 'Savoy' cabbages, globe artichokes and spicy giant red mustard – that's ready to eat. Boiled cabbage seven nights on the trot tries anyone's patience, so last night we tossed together our first spring salad of baby spinach, shredded mint, chives, 'Cos' lettuce, perennial rocket and spring onions. It wasn't anything special but it tasted like spring should.

In another first for the week, I took Lucas on his first trip to a garden centre. It took me so long to get all his gear sorted that we got there five minutes before closing – just long enough for me to cram the car boot with perennials.

Having cleared the weeds out of the two beds at the end of the lawn, Jason dug six huge holes for my new 'Awapuni' cherry trees and, at their feet, I've now planted white *Orlaya grandiflora*, a few cinerarias, babiana bulbs, violets, hellebores, night-scented stock, poppies, pink daisies (*Brachyscome* 'Strawberry Mousse'), dark red knautias and orange-pink *Potentilla* 'Miss Willmott'. The potentillas are tucked between orange- and red-stemmed silverbeet. The colour combination should be cute when they bloom.

We also – finally! – finished planting our bare-root fruit trees down the hill today. (When I say we, I mean that I laid out the trees and then went back up to the house to mind Lucas and bake a chocolate cake while Jason did all the grunt work.)

SEPTEMBER 5: Dramas, dramas! This morning one of our ewes gave birth to twins on a lumpy knoll in the middle of the swamp. I could see she was in trouble from the upstairs bedroom window but my first thought was that she'd snagged her coat in a blackberry thicket and was simply marooned in the mud. I handed Lucas to Maureen and headed down the hill to investigate – and that's when I saw the first lamb wobble to its feet. The second twin, however, was in a bad state.

What a dilemma. Sheep abandon their babies if they sniff so much as a whiff of human intervention but, without my assistance, the lambs would surely have drowned. I tiptoed through the toetoe as quietly as I could, but the ewe saw me coming, panicked, and ploughed into the swamp, leaving her twins high and dry.

We shepherded the deranged mother and the rest of the mob into the big red barn paddock, then I bundled the lambs into Lucas's baby bath, strapped them to the back of the quad bike and delivered them back to their mum. We then circled the mob, Maureen pushing Lucas in his stroller, me doing my best eye dog impersonation, till we enacted a family reunion.

The stronger twin was soon sucking as if its life depended on it, which it did – without that first feed of colostrum, newborn lambs are a lost cause – but its sibling was too weak to lift its head out of the long grass, let alone baa for its mother's attention. I took it home, tucked it into a hand-knitted vest that Lucas had outgrown and popped it into a laundry basket in front of the heat pump. Then I phoned Jason. 'Get to the vet,' I said.

Two hours and 100ml of colostrum later, the lamb was well enough to leap out of the laundry basket and run around the lounge, baaing so loudly it woke Lucas up. My maternal instinct is already stretched a bit thin – I'm busy enough feeding my son every three hours without feeding someone else's – so at nightfall we smuggled the lamb back to its mother. I'll check tomorrow morning to see if she's taken it back.

Incidentally, if the gestation calculator on the Small Kiwi Farms website is accurate, then I was wrong to doubt Rambo's carnal credentials. He must have seduced that ewe on his very first night on our farm.

Kahikateas

Rambo

Seed potatoes

SEPTEMBER 8: Inspired by the flax-flower-stalk tepees in Robert Guyton's Riverton plot, I took my loppers for a stroll in our flax patch this afternoon and made an eco-friendly sweet pea tepee strung together with twine. Around the base I've sown Dr Keith Hammett's 'Patricia Ann' sweet pea blend, which promises old-fashioned, streaky patterned petals in shades of pink, purple, cream and apricot.

Mental note to self: read the seed packet prior to sowing. It says, when sowing a blend of sweet peas, 'select seeds of all sizes, as seeds of darker coloured flowers are often small and shrivelled'. Shame I'd already biffed all the itty-bitty seeds.

SEPTEMBER 9: I'm getting such a kick from keeping my garden on the straight and narrow this season. It's so satisfying to cast an eye over my vege patch, with its tidy rows of transplanted seedlings and trenches of perfectly spaced seed potatoes. I may come to regret it later, when there's a neat strip of weeds between every crop, but for now I'm feeling very industrious. It's much more fun having a tidy garden than a tidy house (which, for the record, I don't).

SEPTEMBER 10: Eight lambs!

SEPTEMBER 11: The weather can't make up its mind. It was picture perfect yesterday but wild, wet and windy today – I was saturated by the time I'd finished planting four bags of seed potatoes ('Cliff's Kidney', 'Ilam Hardy' and a new variety called 'Summer Delight'), two dozen lettuces, three punnets of 'Cheddar' caulis and three punnets of 'Regal Red' cabbages.

I sowed more 'Dwarf Massey' peas and another packet of 'Dwarf Early Green' broad beans – my first pods are almost ready – and I've gone carrot crazy, sowing 26 packets of seed in an experiment for *NZ Gardener*. I've never had much luck growing decent carrots and I usually blame the seed, but I'll have no such excuses this year. I've sown every variety available.

SEPTEMBER 12: Something, or someone, is stealing my marigolds. I slotted them in as row dividers between my carrots, but half of them have been uprooted overnight. Usually I'd point the finger at slugs and snails, but there's no sign of slime. Do Pekin ducks peck at marigolds?

'Pacific Purple' asparagus

FRESH
ASPARAGUS
IS JUICY AND
CRISP AND
SNAPS LIKE A
FRENCH BEAN

SEPTEMBER 16: It's spring! And here's the proof: my first eerie spear of 'Pacific Purple' asparagus, poking out of the soil like a freaky zombie finger.

You're not supposed to pick asparagus for two years, but I got a head start last spring and bought 100 one-year-old crowns from South Island asparagus breeder Dr Peter Falloon. I bedded them in behind the stables in deep trenches lined with blood and bone, sheep manure, compost and straw.

Last spring each crown spawned half a dozen metre-high stems – that's 600 succulent spears, all begging to be cut – but I wasn't the slightest bit tempted. At the time I was so queasy with morning sickness that fresh asparagus – not to mention avocado, cauliflower, tomatoes, red

meat, the sight of raw chicken, and any salad dressing or sauce with even a smidgen of vinegar in it – turned my stomach.

(Onions were the worst though. I couldn't have any in the house, let alone eat them. I had to hold my breath when driving along local roadsides lined with onion weed, *Allium triquetrum*, and – sob! – when my bed of fancy, $5-a-bulb ornamental alliums bloomed, I had to cut off the pom-pom flowers so I could get to our front door without gagging.)

Fresh spring asparagus bears no relation to its canned cousin (although as far as my dad's concerned, if it doesn't come out of a tin and isn't entombed in white bread with the crusts cut off, it isn't actually asparagus). Fresh asparagus is juicy and crisp and snaps like a French bean. It's sweet enough to scoff raw, and tastes of snow pea pods, new potatoes, broccolini and bamboo shoots. It's best eaten within an hour of harvest – as time ticks on, the amputated spears start to cannibalise their own sugar content, converting it to starch.

Lucas helped me pick our first spear, clutching the stalk in his chubby fist as I slipped a knife under the soil to slice it clean from the crown. (I tried to take a photo for posterity – his first harvest! – but at three and a half months, he's as twitchy as a tumbleweed with no will to charm the camera.) We ate it tonight with steamed globe artichokes, a bunch of flowering Chinese cabbage and a bowl of hollandaise sauce. The chooks must know it's spring too: they're finally back on the lay.

Hollandaise sauce

Melt 200g butter. Place 2 egg yolks and 1 tablespoon lemon juice (or cider vinegar) in a metal bowl over a pot of boiling water and whisk constantly until the yolks start to thicken. Gradually dribble in the melted butter, whisking all the time, until the sauce is thick. Season with salt, freshly ground black pepper and a squeeze of lemon juice.

My first asparagus spear, globe artichokes and cherry blossoms

Sprouting kumara

SEPTEMBER 17: Fifteen lambs, including five sets of twins! Rambo looks as deceptively decrepit as crusty old Cecil from Footrot Flats, but he's definitely in working order.

SEPTEMBER 20: The marigold murderer has been unmasked. It wasn't the cats or the chooks or the ducks or the purple swamp hens (you may prefer to call them pukekos). It was *Phasianus colchicus*, an English pheasant. I watched as he ran up the hill, scuttled past the horses in our neighbour Geoff's paddock and sneaked under our fence with his harem of hens close behind. Then, all beaks and feet blazing, I watched them mount an attack on my marigolds, safe in the knowledge that they had the law on their side. The 1953 Wildlife Act says you're only allowed to hunt cocky cock pheasants between May and August (it's illegal to shoot the ladies at all). He'll keep.

SEPTEMBER 23: Whenever my friend Rachel heads north to visit her family at Waimamaku, she brings back a big bag of kumara from Dargaville. I've encouraged one to sprout in my pantry but I won't pick off the runners until I'm sure we've seen the back of Jack Frost.

It's Maori tradition to plant kumara when the shining cuckoo, or pipiwharauroa, comes calling in late spring. It's a beautiful little bird, with a zebra-striped décolletage and a flashy cape of emerald feathers. I've only ever seen one. The poor thing flew into a closed window at Mum and Dad's house. We buried it before the cat could eat it.

SEPTEMBER 24: It's too early to start planting kumara, and it's too early to start sowing beans. But I did anyway today, slipping a packet of 'Borlotto Fire Tongue' seeds around the base of my woven willow obelisks.

Shelled 'Dwarf Early Green'

An heirloom red-seeded broad bean from Nelson

Crimson-flowered broad bean

SEPTEMBER 27: American food activist Michael Pollan has a theory: don't eat anything your grandmother wouldn't recognise on a plate. But I have a better one: don't eat anything your grandmother would recognise, because chances are she habitually boiled it to buggery and scarred your parents' palates for life.

I love broad beans almost as much as my dad loathes them, mostly because I was never forced to eat over-boiled beans as a child. Grandma cooked hers till their skins were grey and rubbery, their flesh floury and dry, prompting Dad to forbid Mum to ever grow them. The result? A gastronomic generation gap. I didn't eat a broad bean until I was in my late twenties.

Broad beans aren't as sexy as shiny aubergines or as succulent as spring asparagus, but in the cool of early spring, when I'm tiring of mashed spuds and cauliflower cheese, they're as dependable and comforting as long johns and flannelette sheets. They're eternal optimists, germinating even in frosty soil and flowering, futilely, from midwinter, when there are no bumblebees around to tickle their cream and charcoal-streaked flowers.

In late autumn I sowed two rows of 'Dwarf Early Green' broad beans and the first pods are now ready to pick. We'll eat them tonight, steamed, skinned, splashed with olive oil and sprinkled with sea salt and shredded mint. If picked early, when the seeds inside those fur-lined pods are no bigger than your thumbnail, they're as sweet as baby peas.

I'm growing rare crimson-flowered broad beans this year too, but not for dinner. I first saw these burgundy beauties at the Chelsea Flower Show a decade ago and have yearned to grow them ever since. The seeds aren't commercially available here and biosecurity regulations make it economically prohibitive to bring them in, but Mark Christensen, a heritage seed saver in Whanganui, has kindly shared half a dozen seeds from his collection. My plants, barely 30cm high, are already in bloom. They're magnificent – or at least as magnificent as a broad bean can be.

I LOVE BROAD BEANS ALMOST AS MUCH AS MY DAD LOATHES THEM

SEPTEMBER 30: Another frost, but I'm not too fussed as my day got off to a sweet start. I've just picked a small bowl of strawberries.

You can never plant too many strawberries. Last autumn I put in 50 bare-root runners and Jason came home today with two dozen potted plants for our new strawberry cages. He's built me two raised beds, each 3 metres by 1 metre, with wooden hinged lids covered in wire mesh to beat the birds. I wanted to pimp them up with custom-made curtain finials but couldn't decide on the shape. Pine cones? Pomegranates? Pineapples? I've settled on two pairs of cast concrete artichokes from a company in Albany. I won't let on to Jason that they cost $50 each.

Strawberry jam

Early in the season, when my strawberries aren't producing enough berries at once for a decent dessert, I pop the fruit into the freezer until I've got enough to make a single jar of jam. Strawberry jam is notoriously reluctant to set, especially if the fruit's overripe, so I use Chelsea's Jam Setting Sugar, which includes pectin.

Method: Mash the fruit with a little water and bring to the boil, then add an equal quantity of jam sugar and boil for 5 minutes. Pour into sterilised jars and seal.

Eton Tidy

We don't eat Eton Mess – that classic English dessert of mashed-up meringues folded into whipped cream with fresh strawberries – in our house. Our version is Eton Tidy.

Method: Slice 500g fresh strawberries, sprinkle with a little sugar and splash with brandy or raspberry vodka (I use our neighbours Greg and Michelle's strawberry liqueur). Set aside for an hour or two, until the berries have softened and released their juices.

Meanwhile, make a batch of meringues. Beat 2 egg whites until stiff. Continue beating, while gradually adding ½ cup caster sugar, until the mixture is thick and glossy. Place spoonfuls onto an oven tray lined with baking paper and bake at 120°C for 1–1½ hours. Set aside to cool.

Whip a bottle of cream, fold in a pottle of strawberry yoghurt, then layer the meringues, macerated berries and cream in tall parfait glasses. Chill until ready to serve.

'Camarosa' strawberries

YOU CAN NEVER PLANT TOO MANY STRAWBERRIES. LAST AUTUMN I PUT IN 50 BARE-ROOT RUNNERS

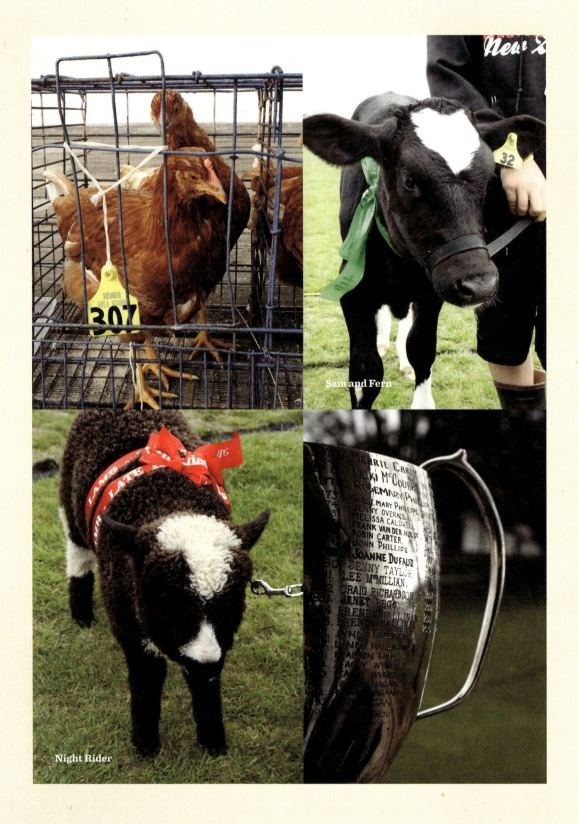

Sam and Fern

Night Rider

OCTOBER 1: On a farm, it pays to avoid getting too attached to your pets. Our parents never made us eat our Calf Club Day champions – the Calf Club champs are the pet lambs and calves – and so my pet lambs were retired to Uncle John's farm in Raglan, and our pet calves went to work for Fonterra. But my nieces' and nephew's pets aren't quite so lucky. My brother-in-law isn't one to get sentimental over a prime leg – or four – of spring lamb.

As a child, I had two pet sheep: Cindy and Cindy. My sister had two Marys. It's safe to say that finding imaginative pet names wasn't our forte. Our family cat was named Biggles; she had a daughter called Littles. We also had a ginger cat called Ginge, and a fat ginger cat called Fatty.

As a child, I also had seven pet calves: Star, Sparkle, Moozi, Liquorice, Lucy, Betty-Lou and Flac. (That's calf spelt backwards. I was running out of ideas by my final year of competition at Calf Club Day.)

Flac was my finest. She had well set ears, straight teeth, an even temper and four good tits (these things matter in the Dairy Type category). I'd brush her coat till it shone, play peek-a-boo behind the pump shed and, on sunny spring days, we'd loll in the long grass together, with not a care in the world.

If you take a pet lamb to Calf Club Day, the hardest category is calling. Lambs are skittish, silly things. Unless they're hungry and think there's a bottle on offer, they usually bolt. But in the calf section, it's the leading competition that requires the most skill. Calves that take fright at the entrance to the obstacle course will simply dig in their hooves and refuse to move.

Flac was an obedient leader and my best shot at getting my name engraved on the champion's trophy – the Hallinan Cup for Leading, donated by Mum and Dad.

On judgement day, Flac didn't put a hoof wrong. We zigzagged through the line of fencing standards, trit-trotted over the bridge and executed a perfect 360 degree turn at the gate. Victory was so close I could smell it, but Flac could smell something else: the freshly mown school athletics field. We were on the home stretch when, without warning, she slumped to her shanks, rolled in the cut grass, and rolled us right out of contention. I remember it as if it was yesterday, though that could be because I've just got home from Onewhero Area School's 2011 Calf Club Day.

The first official Ag Day – an event aimed at fostering a connection between the farming industry and local schoolchildren – was held in Otago in 1911. A century later, it's still going strong in Onewhero. I admired the prize-winning poultry, praised the potato-in-a-bucket winners and cheered a little too loudly when my niece and nephew were competing.

At Calf Club Day this year, there were three Daisys, a Daffodil and at least one All Black. My nephew Sam named his calf Fern, while my niece, Jaime, had a lovely lamb called Snickers. 'Had' being the operative word. Four days ago, Snickers inconveniently expired from bloat.

Poor Jaime was inconsolable. A funeral was hastily convened in the vege patch, Snickers was laid to rest behind the rhubarb and our chubby chocolate ram lamb – now nicknamed Night Rider by the kids – stepped into the breach.

Despite never having worn a lead before in his life, Night Rider led like a shadow. Jaime came first in leading and won a second red sash for rearing. Night Rider was named Reserve Champion. That's my boy!

THE FIRST OFFICIAL AG DAY WAS HELD IN OTAGO IN 1911. A CENTURY LATER, IT'S STILL GOING STRONG

Prunus subhirtella

Prunus subhirtella **blossom**

OCTOBER 3: For weeks the cherry blossom tree by our front door has been spitting out sporadic blossoms, but yesterday it was as if every bud suddenly burst open at once. I'm glad I took a photo of it because, after a ghastly day of gusty winds, there's barely a blossom left on its branches. All the petals are scattered like pink confetti on our deck and driveway. The bees will be disappointed. I've never seen so many honeybees buzzing about in our blossom trees before. The territorial tui who usually scrap over the nectar are keeping a safe distance this year.

OCTOBER 5: We won't be eating strawberries for at least a week. A bloody rat burrowed underneath one of the strawberry cages last night and ate all the ripening berries.

OCTOBER 6: I spent $111.65 before even getting out of bed this morning. I ordered another box of mail order seedlings from Awapuni Nurseries, including two bundles of white campanulas, tall red cornflowers, blue globe thistles (*Echinops ritro*), English daisies, love-in-the-mist, red and white petunias, *Phlox drummondii*, *Phlox* 'Twinkle Star', Shirley poppies, tall Sweet William, 'Cos' lettuces and a bundle each of 'Brandywine Pink' and 'Scoresby Dwarf' tomato seedlings.

OCTOBER 11: I did a double take outside the stables today. The grafted passionfruit vine I bought from Oratia nurseryman Chris Davidson has unfurled its first passionflower for the season.

Chris used to grow passionfruit commercially and came up with the clever idea of grafting his best early and late purple varieties onto the vigorous, disease-resistant rootstock of their cousin the sweet granadilla, *Passiflora ligularis*. The result? Turbo-charged vines that grow – and fruit – at twice the rate of standard passionfruit vines.

My vine has been in for two years but came a cropper last February when Jason held his stag do here. It was a big night. I came home the next day to a mountain of empty beer bottles, a very green-around-the-gills fiancé and green passionfruit littering the ground. At some point during the proceedings, the blokes had taken to pelting each other with them. Boys will be boys – and mine can help me shovel sheep manure around my vine when he gets home today.

(I can't speak highly enough of sheep poo. My late Uncle John, who kept an extensive vegetable garden in Pukekohe, was a lifelong organic gardener. At Pukekapia Primary School, his vegetable bed was twice as productive as those of his contemporaries. His secret? Before leaving for school in the morning, he'd fill his trouser pockets with sheep pellets from the farm to fertilise his plot.)

'Black Beauty' passionflower

I SPENT $111.65 BEFORE EVEN GETTING OUT OF BED THIS MORNING

Capucijner peas

OCTOBER 13: Commercial vegetable growers call October 'the hungry gap' because, despite the daffodils and spring-loaded lambs, the soil's still chilly and growth rates remain glacial. My taste buds are starch-weary and I'm sick of the sight of cabbage, but aside from broad beans, Florence fennel, globe artichokes and asparagus, there's nothing fresh to excite my palate yet – except purple podded peas.

Climbing capucijner peas are a Dutch heirloom dating back to the 1500s, when they were grown by Capuchin monks. Jason's grandfather Fred grew them in his Waipipi garden; his aunts and uncles remember them with varying degrees of fondness.

I saw capucijner peas listed in the Running Brook Seeds catalogue about five years ago and, thinking they were the same as the purple snow peas our family friends Georgie and Paul grow in the UK, sowed a whole packet. I've been saving my own seeds ever since.

Georgie and Paul were enthusiastic English WWOOFers (Willing Workers On Organic Farms) who jacked in their corporate jobs and came to New Zealand to learn how to grow food. They'd only planned to help Uncle John and Aunty Bay in Pukekohe for a fortnight but stayed for six months, before heading home to buy a smallholding in south Devon.

I mention them, not just because of the peas, but because when I visited them a decade ago, they'd just started selling their produce at the Buckfastleigh Farmers' Market. I'd never heard of a farmers' market but I loved what I saw: a group of like-minded growers and farmers setting up stalls in the town square on a Saturday morning to sell pork pies, clotted cream and – in Georgie and Paul's case – punnets of green gooseberries and purple snow peas.

No one here sells true purple mange tout seeds but, if picked young enough, when the pods are still flat and tender, the capucijner is a passable substitute. I've been shelling bowls of my early crop to sauté with onion and bacon or stir through risotto, but the true value of this heritage edible is as a dried pea in bacon hock soups and slow-cooked pork casseroles. I use them instead of store-bought split peas.

The flowers, so pretty in pink and purple, are edible too. I toss them into our salads, though not too many, as each flower picked is a pod sacrificed.

THERE'S NOTHING FRESH TO EXCITE MY PALATE YET – EXCEPT PURPLE PODDED PEAS

Capucijner pea flowers are edible

OCTOBER 14: There's something to be said for planting – and buying – in bulk. With the exception of red-stemmed silverbeet, however. What was I thinking, planting two 3-metre rows of 'Rainbow Lights' beets? We only ever eat silverbeet in vegetarian lasagne and the odd pot of soup. At least our chooks are appreciative. I tie it into bunches to hang from the fruit trees in the orchard and it's hilarious to watch them attack it like a piñata.

Mass-planting is one of the fundamentals of modern garden design but I suspect the concept applies more to flowering perennials and bold foliage plants than edibles. No sane person would want a forest of grapefruit trees or a paddock of courgettes – yet here I am, putting in three more rows of red cabbages, just because I like the look of them.

IF I BUY ONE TREE, I FIGURE I MAY AS WELL BUY 10

If I buy one tree, I figure I might as well buy 10 – it helps to have a burly husband to dig the holes – and if I sow one flower, I might as well sow the whole packet. Last autumn I saw a bulk deal of 100 red tulip bulbs for $72. It seemed extravagant at the time, but they're looking spectacular now.

The only downside to buying bulbs in bulk is having to dig hundreds of tiny holes. When I was invited to visit Prince Charles' private garden at Highgrove a few years ago, he told how he'd ordered 7000 tulip bulbs for his meadow. 'How on earth did you plant them all?' I asked. 'Easy,' he explained. They were divvied up between the team of gardeners and no one was allowed to go home until the job was done!

I tried that tactic on Mum, but by the time we'd planted 150 of the 285 gladioli corms I'd ordered, we'd both lost the will to live. I thanked her for helping and packed her off home to plant the remainder in her own garden.

I've lost count of how many potatoes I've planted. Inspired by all the furrowed fields in the market gardens around Pukekohe, I can't stop digging trenches. I've put in a dozen 1.5kg bags of seed potatoes so far, including 'Jersey Benne', 'Cliff's Kidney', 'Purple Heart', 'Ilam Hardy', 'Moi Moi' and 'Summer Delight'.

It's incredible how quickly everything takes off after a couple of nights of heavy rain, and I'm as pleased as punch with the progress we've made planting around the lawn. But how I wish I'd stood my ground in the discussion my husband and I had over the design. He was adamant that I was not to plant right up to the edge of the stone kerbing. He wanted an access path at the front that was wide enough to push a wheelbarrow down, so we've ended up with an ugly, albeit practical, 40-centimetre strip of bare soil that's slowly filling up with weeds. I'd hoe them in but they're actually self-sown wildflowers from last summer's wedding garden and I'm blowed if I'm going to purposefully pull out free plants, so I'll get my way in the long run.

OCTOBER 15: Turn your back on an asparagus plot at your peril. My asparagus crowns took four weeks to produce their first four spears. But tonight I picked 13 fat stalks – we ate them steamed, with fresh egg pasta, crispy bacon and Parmesan – and there are another 21 spears still out there, waggling their fingers at me disapprovingly. Guess what we'll be having for dinner tomorrow night . . . and the next . . .

'London' tulips

'Pacific Purple' asparagus

Rainbow Lights' silverbeet

Potatoes

OCTOBER 16: Living off the land isn't all raw milk and manuka honey. There are days when I crave my single days and old city ways, swilling champagne in chi-chi cocktail bars and ordering Thai takeaway for dinner. I could still muddle a mojito, I suppose, but I can't make a decent curry. My kaffir lime, cayenne chillis and lemongrass all succumbed after August's freak snowfall.

In the city, the living was easy. The taps never ran dry, there were no possums to raid my roses and Kings Plant Barn was just around the corner. When I lived in the city, the worst thing I ever came home to was a back door bashed in by burglars who'd ransacked my bedroom and pinched all the plonk from my pantry.

In the country, convivial neighbours and kind ladies from the local Country Women's Institute are a greater concern. They turn up unannounced, clutching cakes, invariably catching me still in my pyjamas.

We went visiting ourselves today, though I'll confess to buying a cake at the bakery in Bombay on the way. Our marriage celebrant Danelle has a baby roughly the same age as Lucas, so we caught up for coffee in Pukekohe.

The cows were in the hay paddock below the house, but someone (and it wasn't me which, by the process of elimination, only leaves Jason) hadn't checked that all the gates were latched. Even though the grass was greener on their side of the fence, as soon as we set off on our Sunday drive our 22 heifers hoofed it.

Some of those bovine barbarians were content to prance around the unfenced equestrian arena, nibbling the tips off the 100 European hornbeams (*Carpinus betulus*) I've planted to hedge my fancy formal garden, but the rest moseyed on up the hill. They played Twister in my terraced beds, trampling, with surprising precision, almost all of the 500 Russell lupins I'd painstakingly transplanted from trays. I was trying to replicate Central Otago's rainbow roadsides; it now looks more like a pockmarked lunar landscape.

They ate their way through our new terraced orchard, knocking over the 'Bramley's Seedling' apple trees and stripping the blossoming 'Blackboy' peaches. My quince trees, denuded of every leaf within tongue reach, now sport Dr Seuss-style topknots. The plums were savaged too, though the thorny stems on my all-time favourite ornamental crabapple, *Malus ioensis* 'Plena', saved them from a similar fate.

When we got home, there were six cows tiptoeing through the tulips and one oafish beast had thundered down the lawn and was chewing the chartreuse hem off our finest English oak (*Quercus robur*).

As I surveyed my squashed strawberries and skittled spuds, I tried not to cry. Jason, sensing that my stoic facade was faltering – and possibly fearing spousal abuse – gave me a hug. 'Could've been worse,' he said. He's promised to hire a fencing contractor for my Christmas gift.

AS WE SET OFF ON OUR SUNDAY DRIVE OUR 22 HEIFERS HOOFED IT

OCTOBER 22: Mum phoned this morning from a gala day at Onewhero Area School. 'They're selling vege seedlings for $1 a punnet,' she said. 'Buy the lot,' I said, which explains why I am now digging holes for 48 'Beefsteak' tomato seedlings, two punnets of 'Roma' tomatoes and a banana box filled with leggy lettuces.

I have a theory that tomatoes, like pears, have good years and bad years – but it's anyone's guess which way the season will go. If I do everything by the book – sow the seeds early (August), transplant late (Labour Weekend), sink their roots into compost-enriched soil, stake carefully, pinch out the rampant lateral stems that cause the fruiting trusses to lose focus, pump on the water and feed regularly with potassium-fuelled fertiliser – then I'm almost certain to attract blight, blossom end rot and a plague of stinking green shield beetles. (Meanwhile, a random seedling will sprout in my compost heap and drop 10kg of fruit just to spite me.)

Beginner's luck helps. I had my first, and best, crop of cherry tomatoes in 1997 when I planted a grafted 'Sweet 100' by the door to my rented flat. It grew like a triffid, swallowing an army of stakes as it climbed skyward and tried to weasel its way in through the kitchen window. By summer's end it was 2 metres high by 4 metres wide and as fertile as it was feral. My boyfriend and I ate so many vine-ripened cherry tomatoes that I couldn't face another for five years.

'Sweet 100' is a classic; but buttery yellow 'Sungold' is my favourite sweet cherry type, while 'Black Cherry' is a must-have for meaty, purplish-green fruit. It's the only cherry tomato I've come across that tastes like a proper sandwich tomato, so I grow it every year.

I've planted more tomatoes this year than ever before, because tinned tomatoes are the only canned food (aside from baked beans if Jason's having a bachelor's night) I buy. I chuck a tin of tomatoes into almost every stew and pasta dish I make, so this season I'm determined to grow enough to preserve for winter. All going to plan, I should get a great crop. But then again, I might not.

OCTOBER 23: The All Blacks have won the 2011 Rugby World Cup! The last time they achieved this feat I wrote a gushing letter to All Black captain David Kirk, on whom I had a schoolgirl crush. He replied with an autographed photograph, which I still have to this day. But Richie McCaw's not my type – and who writes letters anyway these days? – so I'm going to celebrate the team's success by planting the all-black petunia 'Black Velvet' instead.

Petunia 'Black Velvet'

OCTOBER 29: A country spring could come with a checklist: bluebells (check), lambs (check), plum blossoms (check), asparagus spears (check), first blowfly sighting (check).

Jason's arranged for Tim Foote – a shearer who works the local lifestyle block round – to whip the wool off our sheep's backs and bums today. Shearing reduces the risk of fly strike and no one – least of all the sheep – wants to deal with a daggy fleece riddled with maggots.

Tim has been shearing Jason's motley flock for a few years. Jason originally got them to keep the grass down around the swamp (if we put cows in there, they'd just eat the trees) and a few of the girls are getting a bit long in the tooth.

We mustered them into the cattle yards and, while Tim stripped them of their wool, Jason docked the lambs' tails and put rubber rings around the boys' bits. Rambo already looks positively wimpish without his wool; the last thing he needs is any aggro from his lively adolescent sons.

One of our oldest ewes has a lovely cocoa and cream coat, so I've separated her fleece into a woolsack in the stables. I'll probably never get around to learning how to spin my own wool, but I would like to have a crack at making felt.

OCTOBER 30: When I moved in with Jason, I came with a city menagerie of three cats and two designer chooks, Sage and Onion. They're fluffy Chinese Silkies.

Onion has gone broody – again. She's sitting on a clutch of 10 eggs, each no bigger than a Cadbury Creme Egg. I'm not convinced that Sage isn't shooting blanks, for this is Onion's third attempt at putting all her eggs into one basket. Not one has ever hatched.

RAMBO LOOKS POSITIVELY WIMPISH WITHOUT HIS WOOL

Onion, my Chinese Silkie hen

OCTOBER 31: Cherry blossom trees are such hussies. These spring trollops, with their seasonal can-can skirts, are all talk. When their blossoms drop, I never did see a duller tree. Give me an apple any day. *Malus* blossom is beauty with a purpose.

An apple orchard in blossom is a joyous sight to behold, and Lucas and I have started to behold ours on our morning constitutionals. It takes a bit of effort to tucker out a five-and-a-half-month-old between feeds, but we've worked out a routine. We feed the chooks and the ducks, fondle the fuzzy nubs developing on the almond trees, investigate what's germinating in the plastic house, kick the ball up the lawn for the dogs, walk down the driveway to get the mail and walk back through the apple and pear orchard.

The pears are always last to blossom but the apples are in full bloom now, their whippy boughs studded with fuchsia buds that open to pale petals stained ever so slightly pink. Apple blossoms are edible, did you know? Having discovered this fact on the internet yesterday, I nibbled my way through a bowl of them this morning in a bid to put my finger on the exact flavour. They taste nicer than nasturtiums, though I still can't describe quite how they taste without sounding like a wine industry tosser. I can detect floral notes, a hint of grass and cherry guava, and a slight citrus chaser.

In Riverton, my *NZ Gardener* colleague Robert Guyton and his wife Robyn have been collecting apple trees from old Southland orchards in a bid to catalogue the region's heirlooms before they're lost. They now have more than 300 trees growing in a trial block out the back of Marshwood Gardens in Invercargill. (Owner

I NIBBLED MY WAY THROUGH A BOWL OF APPLE BLOSSOMS THIS MORNING

Geoff Genge is another top bloke from the deep south; my *Nicotiana mutabilis* plants came from his mail order nursery.)

I was talking to Robert this morning. He says native kereru or, as he calls them, 'rats of the skies', have been a menace to his plums this spring, eating the buds before they get the chance to open. (No such problems here – my plum trees are a mass of blossom.)

I got quite jealous when Robert told me he was planning a blossom party in his heritage apple orchard. 'We'll wear floppy hats and drink to excess (I hope!), frolic about and admire the pinks and whites. The invitees have to bring a bag of manure to deposit at the base of their favourite tree, so it'll be a curious sort of event,' he reckons.

Apple blossoms are appealing in a vase too, but I'm loath to cut any to bring indoors. In Roman times, apple boughs were hung over the marital bed to help couples conceive but, as much as I love wee Lucas, I'm not ready to give him a brother or sister just yet.

The only fruit tree more exquisite than an apple in full bloom is the handsome quince, *Cydonia oblonga*. Its elegant single blossoms are tinted sugar-pink – Martha Stewart has even named a paint colour after them – but what sets them apart is their size. While most fruit trees have petite blossoms, and plenty of them, the quince has proper flowers, each boasting five big cupped petals around a cluster of fat stamens. Pear trees are often grafted onto quince rootstock, which is why in old farm gardens you often see gnarled pear trees sporting the odd branch of quinces.

Quince blossom

Cherry blossom

Crabapple blossom

pple blossom

NOVEMBER 4: Success in a vege patch is easy to gauge – if you don't go hungry, you've got it right – but I have higher expectations for my flower garden. I want a cheerful and continuous display outdoors, plus enough blooms to fill every vase indoors.

I've nailed it this spring. For starters, I'm filling jugs with fragrant cream freesias. Now there's a smell to transport me back to my childhood! Freesias must have been made of tougher stuff back then, for I remember them effortlessly erupting into bloom every year along the side of Mum's vege patch, whereas mine are one-hit wonders that require replanting every year.

My rose garden teeters on the precipice of spring perfection. It's full of promise, and sultry, swelling buds. The old gallica 'Rosa Mundi', named for Henry II's mistress Rosamund Clifford, is already in full bloom, with crimson-streaked petals that remind me of boysenberry ripple ice cream. It's surrounded by a cloud of pink and white *Nicotiana sylvestris*, plus baskets of dwarf 'Vera' bougainvilleas and charming two-toned 'Taffy' penstemons. It's all terribly girly.

I never did get around to staking the 'Wiltshire Ripple' sweet peas planted along the length of the asparagus bed. They're a big tangled mess, but soon they'll be a big tangled mess of scented blooms, so I don't mind.

Elsewhere in the garden I have radiant lilac rhododendrons, 'Tickled Pink' perennial petunias, pink cosmos, dwarf blue delphiniums and swathes of self-sown *Silene armeria* (an annual catchfly with the charming common name of 'none-so-pretty') from last summer's wildflower border.

I've also got a television crew standing in the middle of my crop of cabbages. I'm presenting a series of gardening segments on the Living Channel and they couldn't have picked a prettier time of the year to film. It is, at long last, absolutely, positively, unequivocally spring, even if snow is being forecast for alpine parts of the South Island.

Nicotiana mutabilis

'Rosa Mundi'

Blue larkspurs

Pink cosmos

Penstemons and a basket of dwarf 'Vera' bougainvilleas

NOVEMBER 6: Poppies are popping up everywhere. I have more self-sown soldier poppies (*Papaver rhoeas*) than a Flanders field, plus full-skirted Shirley poppies, crinkled Iceland poppies (*Papaver nudicaule*), fluffy peony poppies (*Papaver paeoniflorum*), red opium poppies (*Papaver somniferum*) and Oriental poppies (*Papaver orientale*) with buds as fat as chicken drumsticks.

No other flower appears as fragile as the poppy, but looks are deceiving. The paper-thin petals of *Papaver nudicaule* aren't the least bit fazed by frost. Mine have been flowering since August. They last several days in a vase too, though I have to singe their stems with the chef's professional blow torch I bought Jason.

When my poppies have finished flowering, I won't pull them out. I'll let most of the pods swell and burst, scattering seed for next spring, then I'll shake the rest into a container for my spice rack. Opium poppy seeds are the best for baking, but they're also jolly hard to come by (MAF changed the importation rules a couple of years ago, which has seen them all but disappear from local seed catalogues), so I use peony poppy seeds in my muffins instead.

NOVEMBER 5: Jason has come over all territorial about our potato tubers. He seems to think that, because he dug the trenches, they're his jurisdiction. But when he wasn't looking this afternoon, I snuck out with the spade and dug up the last 'Jersey Benne' plant in the row closest to our house. The tops have only just started to flower so I was thrilled to unearth eight waxy new potatoes. We boiled them with sprigs of fresh mint and ate them straight out of the pot, along with half a dozen pink-jacketed 'Desiree' potatoes. These third-generation self-sown sprogs keep coming up in my asparagus bed. I thought I'd defeated them last summer, but I was wrong. At least they gave us a free feed.

Citrus poppy seed muffins
This dead-easy recipe comes from the Chelsea Sugar website.

Method: Preheat oven to 200°C. Combine 2 cups self-raising flour, 1 cup sugar and ½ cup poppy seeds (the yield from 3–4 perennial poppy plants) with the finely grated zest of 2 citrus fruit. In a second bowl, whisk together 100g butter, melted, 1 cup milk and 2 eggs. Fold liquid into dry ingredients. Don't overmix. Spoon into a 12-tin muffin tray and bake for 10–15 minutes. While the muffins are cooking, squeeze the juice from 2 citrus fruit and mix with ¼ cup sugar. Spoon this glaze over the muffins as soon as you pop them out of the tins.

Double Shirley poppy

Soldier poppies

Red opium poppy

Single Shirley poppy

Papaver 'Ladybird'

NOVEMBER 7: I counted 79 asparagus spears this morning. Truth be told, I'm sick of the sight of them. I'd intended to sell my asparagus crop at the Clevedon Farmers' Market but I've been too busy juggling other weekend work commitments to get there yet.

I thought I could start preserving some but when I googled 'bottling asparagus' it turned up a cautionary tale about bottling botulism instead. On the website of the US National Library of Medicine's National Center for Biotechnology Information, I came across a report from 1948, which revealed in considerable detail the unfortunate deaths of two people (and countless chickens) on a Canadian farm. I read the highlights to Jason:

Just before noon on February 23, 1948, a farmer had a hurried lunch with his wife and daughter. The meal consisted of soup, veal, potatoes, asparagus, bread, cake and tea. The man had fetched a bottle of asparagus from the basement at his wife's request. After warming the contents in a frying pan, she had served a helping to each person, and poured the remainder into a dish which was placed on the table. The man was a light eater, and did not have a second helping of asparagus; but the women were both heavy eaters, the wife weighing 260lb.

After breakfast next day, the wife complained of a pain in her side. The daughter, who had left home the night before to return to work at a hotel in town, had a bad headache on rising that

morning. The farmer went outside to do a few chores, and noticed several chickens sitting on the roost 'as if they were drunk'.

Their condition rapidly worsened . . . The mother died and the daughter 20 minutes later, 50 hours after eating the asparagus. The sick chickens, some 10 in all, had also died.

The information suggested botulism as the possible cause of death . . . Police were requested to forward any homecanned foodstuffs found on the premises. A consignment was received, comprising two sealers of meat, one of string beans, two of corn, one of corn on the cob, one of tomatoes and three of asparagus. On removal of the lids, all the bottles appeared tightly sealed, except one of meat, and the three of asparagus. A lesson to be drawn from these fatalities is the need for continued education of the public in home-preservation of foodstuffs. The farmer recalled having helped his wife perform the bottling nine months prior to the fatalities. The asparagus had been brought in from the field, washed, placed in an open kettle on the stove, and boiled until 'cooked through'. The bottles were just washed in warm water by the woman, the asparagus filled into the bottles, and the tops put on by the man. There was no subsequent heating. This almost unbelievably casual technique obviously afforded plenty of opportunity for contamination from soiled fingers during filling and capping of the bottles. In view of the very slovenly bottling process,

WHEN I GOOGLED 'BOTTLING ASPARAGUS' IT TURNED UP A CAUTIONARY TALE ABOUT BOTTLING BOTULISM

it is rather astonishing that Clostridium botulinum should have been present in only two of the bottles.

Two points, viz., the death of the chickens, and the farmer's escape from botulism, may be readily explained, although on circumstantial evidence only. The man recalled having let the chickens out of the run as he left home after the fatal lunch. They were apt to stay around the house, and his wife customarily fed them scraps from the household meals. The man's failure to contract botulism may probably be ascribed to his comparatively small appetite, and to the fact that his portion may have been heated to a higher temperature in the frying pan. After he had left, the women perhaps ate the remaining asparagus, some portion of which may not have been even warmed in the pan.

Another possibility is that they had tasted the asparagus on first opening the bottle, before it was warmed; for the husband stated that his wife's preserved foodstuffs had frequently gone bad, and she was in the habit of tasting them before serving.

I've officially, though quietly (much too quietly for him to hear), appointed Jason as chief preserve taster in our relationship.

'Pacific Purple' asparagus

Potatoes, kale and carrots

Nasturtium 'Peach Melba'

Calendula

Bidens ferulifolia 'Flair'

NOVEMBER 8: Yellow is my least favourite colour. I used to love it – the first rose I ever planted was golden 'Eldorado' – but now I loathe it. Aside from daffodils, courgettes, tomatoes, pumpkins, Jerusalem artichokes and a cute new dwarf daisy, *Bidens ferulifolia* 'Flair', I haven't intentionally planted anything yellow-flowered for yonks. Even the sunflowers I sowed as a backdrop for our wedding weren't yellow. I chose the bronze and mahogany varieties 'Moulin Rouge' and 'Evening Sun'.

I'm not too keen on orange either, aside from the Mexican sunflower, *Tithonia speciosa* 'Goldfinger', calendulas and wanton wandering nasturtiums with scarlet-orange petals. 'Empress of India' has long been my favourite nasturtium but this year I'm rather captivated by quaint clumps of 'Peach Melba' too. The flowers are more mango than peach, with orange streaks.

Organic gardeners swear by nasturtiums as companion plants to repel bugs from fruit trees, tomatoes, cabbages and cucumbers, but I grow them largely for their good looks as gap-fillers between boring-looking crops like spinach and silverbeet. Unlike the colonising nasturtiums of old, the 'Empress' and 'Peach Melba' are clumping types with good manners and no desire to travel. Plus their flowers and baby leaves add an appetising zing to spring salads and, when pickled, the peppery seed pods are a passable substitute for capers.

NOVEMBER 13: There was a young girl, Lily, selling avocados for $1 each at the Clevedon Farmers' Market this morning. I bought five, though I don't need any. I've rather gone off them since reading that an avocado has the same number of calories as 10 teaspoons of butter or 5 tablespoons of peanut butter.

Lucas likes mashed avocado, though to be honest he's far more interested in mauling the unripe fruit on his play mat. For every teaspoon he eats, I eat the rest. At this rate, I'll never fit my pre-pregnancy jeans again.

ORGANIC GARDENERS SWEAR BY NASTURTIUMS AS COMPANION PLANTS TO REPEL BUGS. I GROW THEM LARGELY FOR THEIR GOOD LOOKS

NOVEMBER 15: Peas, potatoes, sweetcorn, strawberries and 'Scarlet Runner' beans: these are the crops I clearly recall my sister and I helping Mum harvest from her vegetable garden on the farm. More strawberries ended up in our mouths than ever made it to the bowl and, as soon as our fingers were nimble enough to split their seams, we preferred to pilfer fresh peas from the pod than shell them into a colander.

I haven't always been partial to peas. As a three-year-old, I caused quite a scene at my Aunt Dorothy's dinner table when I was refused permission to leave until I'd cleared my plate of peas. I sulkily did as I was told, then hurled the lot back in a remarkable impersonation of that infamous scene from *The Exorcist*. (A film, I hasten to add, that gave me nightmares for a week when I watched it on television, through a crack in the lounge door, without my parents' knowledge.)

I HAVEN'T ALWAYS BEEN PARTIAL TO PEAS

I'm not sure why I had such an early aversion to peas. I adore them now. I consider it a mark of success if I can pick enough pods at any one time to make a proper meal, though I'm equally happy simply to snack on them as I work in the garden.

My fail-safe pea is 'Dwarf Massey', but this season I've sown the gutsy climbing 'Onward' as well. Its puffy pods are a marvel – they're packed with peas that are twice as big, their flavour twice as sweet, as their dinky dwarf cousins.

Risi e bisi (Rice and pea soup)

This Venetian classic is my 'chicken soup for the soul', sans chook, for cold spring nights when I feel like comfort food but can't face another plate of starchy spuds. Risi e bisi is traditionally served as a soup, but I make mine more like a sloppy risotto – which funnily enough, is usually how my risotto turns out as well!

Risi e bisi is best with the season's first baby peas, shelled straight into the soup pot, though frozen peas are fine too. I add fresh peas a minute or two before serving, so they're barely cooked through but full of flavour. If using frozen peas, add them at the same time as the second measure of stock.

I've been making this for years. I came across the original recipe in one of Antonio Carluccio's early cookbooks and, like most Italian classics, no precise measurements are required.

Method: Finely dice a small onion (add celery too if you have it). In a medium-sized soup pot, heat a generous glug of olive oil and sauté the onion over a low heat with the lid on until it's translucent. Add 1 cup arborio rice and stir until it's coated in oil, then pour in 2 cups good quality hot chicken stock and 1 cup white wine. Simmer, covered, for about 10 minutes, allowing the rice to absorb most of the stock, then ladle in another 2 cups hot stock. Simmer until the rice is tender then add 1 cup of fresh baby peas. Season with salt and freshly ground black pepper and ladle into bowls, topped with a pile of freshly grated Parmesan.

'Dwarf Massey' and capucijner peas

NOVEMBER 18: I love this time of the year, even though I get next to nothing done, indoors or out. When Lucas is asleep, I head into the garden with the best of intentions to weed, prune, plant and sow . . . only to find myself wandering about absent-mindedly snipping sweet peas, tickling the wayward tendrils of my hop vines back into line, or sinking my nose deep into David Austin's most fragrant roses.

I don't see the point of roses without scent, just as I don't see the point of a garden without roses. I'm not talking about those prissy hybrid teas and fancy floribundas either. I've gone for a mix of voluptuous modern English roses and old-fashioned heritage roses that ooze history and have intoxicating, biblical-sounding scents like myrrh and musk.

I DON'T SEE THE POINT OF A GARDEN WITHOUT ROSES

There were a number of roses in the garden when I moved here, and I've retained all the ones that I liked, though – like the house – they've been shuffled into new positions. (Two weeks after I met Jason, he hired a crane and hauled his teeny-tiny 70-square-metre house 35 metres to the west to clear a building site for a new dwelling. I put paid to that plan by suggesting, instead, a huge garden with a cricket-pitch-sized formal lawn edged with stone kerbing. Will we build a bigger house in the future? And ruin my $3000 lawn? I think not.)

I've planted two dozen roses in a 3 metre-wide rock-walled bed that runs the length of the stables. When it's time to prune, I start at one end and work my way, painfully, to the other. The bed's far too deep to be practical. By late spring it's impossible to fight through the thorny canes to whip out any weeds or stake my dahlias and by the end of summer I have to employ long-handled loppers to clear an access route through the middle. But for now, it's sensational.

I made another rather amateur error when ordering my roses. I scoured the Trinity Farm and Tasman Bay Rose catalogues for flowers in pale pink, dark pink, striped pink and deep burgundy, but now that they're in bloom, I can't tell my 'Charles de Mills' from my 'Chianti'. At least there's no confusing 'William Shakespeare 2000' with 'William Lobb'. The latter is a heritage moss rose and sports stems and buds with a peculiar coat of stubble that's often mistaken for a severe infestation of aphids.

My rose garden

A tussie-mussie

'radescant'

Roses with white orlaya

'Noble Antony'

'Tess of the d'Urbervilles'

'Veilchenblau'

MY FAVOURITE ROSE?

Whatever's in bloom on the day, or so any true rosarian will tell you, though I've narrowed it down to my top 10.

1. 'Charles de Mills'. A gallant, gorgeous, dark crimson gallica with flowers that open so flat you could be forgiven for thinking they'd been sandwiched between the pages of a book. And the perfume! Of all my dark roses, this one is to die for. But then, so too are 'Prospero', 'Falstaff', 'Tradescant', 'Chianti' and 'William Shakespeare 2000'.

2. 'Tess of the d'Urbervilles'. This is the first David Austin to bloom in my garden each spring, with large, lovely, full-petalled blooms on prickly stems. The first flush is deep crimson-pink, but its summer blooms are smaller and dark red.

3. 'Chevy Chase'. A climber with buttonhole blooms, but masses of them, in a deliciously vibrant shade of dark red/pink. It's dead easy to strike from cuttings too.

4. Rosa centifolia. This intensely fragrant, hundred-petalled rose is unrivalled for romantics (and the Dutch masters), despite its unfortunate common name of cabbage rose.

5. 'Gertrude Jekyll'. Gertie, as David Austin's staff fondly call her, is a pink lady with panache and perfume. My all-time favourite pink rose? Perhaps, though, it's a toss up between her and the luscious bourbon 'Mme Isaac Pereire'.

6. 'Brother Cadfael'. The first time I saw – and smelled – this luscious David Austin rose was at the Scented Rose Garden in Tasmania's Huon Valley. Its cupped, pale pink blooms are the colour of fairground candyfloss and as big as peonies, with a full-on fragrance to match. It's a dead ringer for 'Heritage', which I also grow.

7. 'Raubritter'. Can a rose be cute? 'Raubritter' is. In spring this sprawling shrub rose is smothered in clusters of cupped pink pixie-sized flowers.

'William Lobb'

'Variegata di Bologna'

'Wedding Day'

8. 'Variegata di Bologna'. I love it, like 'Rosa Mundi' and 'Camaieux', for its striped candy cane blooms of red and white. But honestly, it's a mongrel. I don't spray my roses and every summer 'Variegata di Bologna' gets such bad black spot on its matt green leaves that it would technically be more accurate to describe it as having matt green spots on black leaves.

9. 'Wedding Day'. This once-blooming rambler is perversely unromantic in nature. It's a thug with a marvellously marketable moniker. 'Wedding Day' was already in the garden and is at least 8 metres tall. Having clambered up one of the liquidambars, it flings its white veil from the treetops for four weeks in late spring.

10. 'Roseraie de l'Hay'. My pick of the possum-proof prickly rugosas, this tough but beautiful rose has ruffled blooms of deep crimson-purple and a sweet, spicy perfume. I equally adore 'Scabrosa', 'Hansa' and the white 'Blanc Double de Coubert'.

Did I say 10? I lied. I also wouldn't be without 'Gloire de Guilan', 'Veilchenblau', 'Mary Rose', 'Jean Ducher' and 'English Elegance', though I wish I hadn't let my heart rule my credit card when I ordered six bushes of the almost black-red 'Astrid Grafin von Hardenberg'. Released here in 2010 and named Most Fragrant Rose at the 2011 New Zealand Rose of the Year awards, it was love at first sight. I raved evangelically about her to Paul Holmes on his radio show, promising to send him a plant. I'm so pleased I didn't. Ours was a fleeting affair: Astrid's actually a bit of a dog. The flowers rarely reach their potential, as the dark outer petals brown off before the blooms have fully opened. I'm prepared to make allowances for prima donna behaviour, but I've no time for poor performers. My plants are destined for the compost heap.

'Cheddar' and 'Green Macerata' cauliflowers

NOVEMBER 20: My vege garden is going great guns. I've planted far too much. It doesn't help that the brassicas Mum planted the week before Lucas was born are suddenly as big as basketballs. No amount of huffing and puffing on my part can prise them from the soil. I've had to ask Jason to decapitate them with his hand saw.

A colossal cauliflower is both a blessing and a burden. The first one we picked weighed 4kg. The damn thing wouldn't fit in the fridge.

I hacked it to bits but the florets still filled both vege crisper bins, even after I fobbed some off on Mum.

We've had cauliflower – either raw in a salad, steamed or drowned in cheese sauce – for five nights in a row, and there's still a quarter left in the fridge. Or at least there was until a few minutes ago. Having waited until Jason was asleep, I snuck outside and flung the rest of the damn thing to the chooks.

WE'VE HAD CAULIFLOWER – EITHER RAW IN A SALAD, STEAMED OR DROWNED IN CHEESE SAUCE – FOR FIVE NIGHTS IN A ROW

NOVEMBER 26: I'm as excited as a child on Christmas Eve. I've booked my first stall at the Clevedon Farmers' Market for tomorrow morning.

When I lived in the city, I sold my excess crops at the City Farmers' Market at Britomart and the Grey Lynn Farmers' Market. I even once hopped down the line to the Hamilton Farmers' Market when I had a surfeit of Jerusalem artichokes and no hope of eating them all. But the Clevedon Farmers' Market is my local. I could be a tad biased, but I also think it's the best Auckland market, offering everything from pickled figs and paella to pony rides and organic potatoes.

MY POTATO HARVEST IS SHAPING UP TO BE A CRACKER OF A CHRISTMAS CROP

It's only 17 kilometres from Hunua. Jason and I went there on our second date. I knew he was the man for me when, an hour later, he agreed to accompany me to the Clevedon Valley Buffalo Company's farm to pat their goofy-looking newborn calves. Most men would have written me off as slightly – only slightly? – obsessive.

We all have different dreams: some kids want to be astronauts, or firefighters, or fairy princesses. I just wanted to live on a busy road. I wanted a roadside stall where I could sell homemade lemonade, like the girls in the American story books I devoured; or bags of 'Shiny Fardenlosa' beans, like Uncle John.

We lived on the main road in Onewhero, but that wasn't saying much. Beyond our gate, there weren't many houses on the loop road to Wairamarama and back (an hour's round trip

if you showed any cheek to Brucie the school bus driver).

It has taken me all day to prepare for the market. I've shaken the slugs out of my cauliflowers, stacked up my asparagus spears and dug up seven rows of spray-free spuds.

My potato harvest is shaping up to be a cracker of a Christmas crop. For every 1.5kg bag of 'Jersey Benne' seed potatoes I planted, I'm averaging an 11kg yield.

My two rows of 'Purple Heart' have yielded 24kg, with tubers averaging between 200 and 250g. Not a bad haul, except these big, dark spuds are so hard to see in the soil that I impaled all the best ones with my fork.

My 'Cliff's Kidney' crop looked unpromising. The tops weren't as large or healthy-looking as the 'Jersey Bennes', and I didn't mound them up as well as I should. Even so, when I started digging, I soon discovered that they'd bred like rabbits. Each plant averaged 10 to 15 oval tubers and, though they were generally smaller than the 'Jersey Bennes', the largest individual spud weighed 300g. Average yield? A hearty 14kg.

But the pick of the crop so far is 'Summer Delight', a new variety. I can't fault this good-sized, yellow-fleshed, oval-shaped, all-purpose spud. Robust and vigorous, my plants are twice as big as the neighbouring crop of 'Cliff's Kidney', despite having been planted a month later. Each row yielded 16kg.

We've dug so many spuds that every basket I own is full of them. It took me all evening – during which I downed most of a bottle of sauvignon blanc – to gently wash the dirt off them. At 11 p.m., I was seriously contemplating piling the last load into the washing machine (delicate cycle, of course) when Jason intervened.

'Surely people are capable of washing their own potatoes?' he said. 'Come to bed.'

Cliff's Kidney' potatoes

Jason and Lucas

NOVEMBER 27: I needn't have bothered washing those spuds. They sold so quickly I didn't even get the chance to pop them all into the brown paper bags I'd prepared with charming Foggydale Farm labels designed by my friend Olivia. By 10 a.m., I'd sold 76kg – and could have sold more if I'd had them. Luckily it's only a half-hour round trip from the market to our garden, so I sent Jason home to dig up another four rows. We sold all those too. By 11 a.m. everything was gone – aside from two 'Savoy' cabbages and five globe artichokes – so from then on I offered free gardening advice instead.

My stand may not have been the most profitable, given my teething problems with supply and demand, but by golly it was pretty! I recycled some of the fabric bunting that Mum made for our wedding and Jason begrudgingly lugged along my own wooden table (I knew that impulse buy from Vintage Antiques and Collectables in Nelson would come in handy one day). I dusted off the old apple crates in the stables, polished my green kitchen scales, slipped my hand-tied tussie-mussies and sweet pea posies into Agee jars, and displayed the rest of my wares in wicker baskets. It all looked so lovely that I was loath to sell any of it. I didn't want to ruin the display.

I suspect I'll need a slightly more ruthless retail strategy if this market adventure is to pay its way. If I factor in the six hours of preparation and knock off my expenses (two cupcakes, two mochaccinos and a bambino ciabatta for Lucas to chew on), I'd be lucky to have earned the minimum wage for my morning's efforts. But money isn't everything. I had a blast . . . and I can't wait to go back.

BY 10 A.M.,
I'D SOLD
76KG – AND
COULD HAVE
SOLD MORE
IF I'D HAD
THEM

'Purple Heart' potatoes

MY STAND
MAY NOT
HAVE BEEN
THE MOST
PROFITABLE
. . . BUT BY
GOLLY IT WAS
PRETTY

❧

I'm holding my first crop of 'Summer Delight' potatoes

NOVEMBER 28: Onion, I've reluctantly conceded, is sitting on dud eggs again. I've taken them off her before they start self-combusting like stink bombs. Rotorua has nothing on a real rotten egg.

While Onion has been broody, our other chooks have been busy. They're cranking out so many eggs that I've been forced to stack them, Jenga-style, inside the fridge. I'm fast running out of room, and patience for cleaning up the ones that invariably topple out onto the floor when I open the fridge door too quickly, so I've bought an ice cream machine. I have a recipe for vanilla ice cream that uses five eggs.

I started with a batch of plum sorbet (I had to thaw the last of last summer's 'Damsons' in order to make space in our freezer to pre-chill the ice cream machine's churning bowl) and a raspberry slushy. I didn't read the instructions properly. The machine has to go back into the freezer for 24 hours between each batch.

I wish I could make a frozen gooseberry fool, but the prickly plants I've grown from cuttings from a Queenstown gardener aren't yet fruiting. I could ask my Aunt Jackie to ship me a box I suppose. She's selling them for $5 per kg at the Oxford Farmers' Market. They fetch $5 per punnet up here.

Dad loves gooseberry pie. As a child, he remembers top-and-tailing them by the

Fruit sorbet

Start by making a simple sugar syrup. Bring 100g caster sugar to boil in 1 cup water, stirring until dissolved. Take off the heat and cool, then combine with a squeeze of lemon juice and 2 cups fruit purée — try raspberries, strawberries, peaches, apricots or plums. Cook the fruit in a little water till soft, purée in a food processor or blender, strain if desired, then chill overnight before you churn it.

Homemade vanilla ice cream

In a small pot, gently heat 500ml full cream milk, 300ml cream, a pinch of salt, ½ cup sugar and 1 teaspoon vanilla paste (or a split vanilla pod) until it reaches a slow simmer.

Meanwhile, beat 5 egg yolks (make meringues with the whites) with ½ cup sugar until the mixture is pale and fluffy.

Take the cream mixture off the heat and gradually pour half into the egg mixture, whisking constantly. Then pour it all back into the pot and reheat slowly (don't let it boil), stirring constantly, until it thickens enough to coat the back of a spoon. Pour into a bowl, cool to room temperature, then chill overnight. Twenty minutes of churning later, you've got a tub of gourmet vanilla-bean ice cream.

thousand before they went into the pot. It didn't put him off.

My Australian cousins in tropical Queensland have never encountered a fresh gooseberry in a garden. I had to chuckle when they mistook the balloon-shaped seed pods on my love-in-a-mist plants (*Nigella damascena*) for green gooseberries. I can't imagine they'd make for a very nice pie, though nigella seeds are edible. *Nigella sativa*, a slightly less ornamental species than *Nigella damascena*, is the source of the spice black cumin.

NOVEMBER 30: We had 10,000 litres of water delivered today. Jason has rigged up a petrol-powered irrigation system, with a set of industrial nozzles that spray my crops at fire-hose strength. I gave the garden a mighty good soak tonight and accidentally drained the tank again. I'm now recycling Lucas's bath water to revive the parched seedlings in my propagating house. Nothing says summer's here like an empty tank.

Plum sorbet

SUMMER

There's nowhere I'd rather be
than in my garden in summer,
reaping what I've sown.

Dahlia 'Oreti Bimbo'

Sweet peas

My cottage border

Queen Anne's lace

Calendulas and everlasting daisies

Elderflowers

SUMMER'S HERE, EVEN IF THERE'S NO SIGN OF ANY SUN.

It's not balmy enough to break out my sundresses and sandals yet, but my garden looks like it's clothed in Liberty fabric. How did it get so feminine? Everywhere I look there's dainty gypsophila, Queen Anne's lace, scented sweet peas, Sweet William, honeywort and love-in-the-mist.

———— •((•))• ————

DECEMBER 1: There's an elderberry tree (*Sambucus nigra*) on the main drag out of Tuakau that seems forever in flower. This afternoon I picked a bag of blooms to make elderflower champagne for Christmas – it takes at least two weeks to work up a decent fizz.

Though I make elderflower cordial and elderflower champagne every summer, I'm still not entirely sure I like the taste. Elderflower blossoms have a slightly bilious undertone, like Rose's Lime Cordial, and a grassy, sauvignon blanc-style fragrance. In Nigel Slater's *Tender Volume II*, my all-time favourite fruit cookery book (it's beaten only by his vegetable-themed tome, *Tender Volume I*), he describes their smell as 'the essence of the English summer Miss Marple might have known. Of cricket matches and policemen on bikes, village greens and shady, leafy lanes. On a less romantic note, I detect a hint of fresh yeast and tomcats.'

I know elders are disgraceful weeds in the deep south, but as far as I'm concerned these are punks with a purpose. How many other weeds boast delicate blossoms to dip into pikelet batter as well as purple berries for autumn jams and jellies? Even the toxic foliage has its uses. Like rhubarb leaves, it can be turned into a natural insecticide to tackle aphids on roses. Simply simmer 500g of elder leaves in 5 litres of water for half an hour, let it cool, then strain, add a squirt of dishwashing detergent and spray.

Elderflower cordial

I once made elderflower cordial on a cruise ship in Croatia. The chef was none too pleased when I returned from a day trip to the island of Mljet with a bag of blossoms to boil up, but they certainly improved the flavour of the cheap wine we were drinking!

Method: On a sunny day, pick 25 fully open elderflower heads. Shake off any bugs and place the flowers in a large bowl with the rind of 2 lemons. In a pot, bring 2kg sugar, 1.5 litres water and the juice of 2 lemons to the boil; take off heat and add 1 tablespoon citric acid. Pour the syrup over the elderflowers, cover and stand overnight. In the morning, strain through muslin cloth and bottle. Dilute to taste.

Elderflower champagne

Pour 10 litres boiling water into a clean plastic bucket and cool to room temperature. Add juice and rind of 2 lemons, 1kg sugar and ¼ cup cider or white wine vinegar. Trim the stalks off at least 20 large elderflower heads and submerge. Add a pinch of baker's yeast to kick-start gentle fermentation. Cover the bucket and stand it in a warm room for 2–3 days, stirring occasionally. Strain it and bottle.

Or try this cheat's method from Christchurch gardeners John and Margaret Webb. Buy a bottle of Schweppes Classic Dry Lemonade. Take a good swig out of the bottle, stuff in half a dozen elderflowers and screw the cap back on. Shake gently and stand overnight. Chill. Instant elderflower fizz!

DECEMBER 3: My friend Peter has nicked me a bag of green walnuts from his neighbour's tree. I'll use them to make nocino, an Italian green walnut liqueur that ages to the colour of a strong long black and tastes as smooth as liquid cinnamon.

The traditional recipe calls for 29 adolescent walnuts and a barefoot virgin to pluck them straight from the lowest boughs. The best I can do is think pure thoughts as I carefully quarter the unripe nuts with a meat cleaver. The shells inside the green husks should be soft enough to slice through without any resistance; if the knife hits a hard shell, it means I've left it too late in the season.

The first time I made nocino, I didn't know that cut walnuts stain your hands black. By the time I'd finished chopping them, I looked like I'd strangled a squid – and no amount of scrubbing would lift the colour. I wear rubber gloves for the job now.

DECEMBER 4: It's lucky I like coleslaw because I got rather carried away growing carrots, purple cabbages and fat-bottomed 'Early Purple Vienna' kohlrabi this season. I have an excuse for the carrots – it's a trial for *NZ Gardener* magazine – but what on earth possessed me to plant so many brassicas? Even if we eat kohlrabi every night until Christmas we haven't a hope of eating it all.

Kohlrabi's a quirky beast. Its base swells like a bee sting and sits shy of the soil. The flavour's reminiscent of raw cabbage or broccolini but with the waxy texture of a new potato. I cube it into curries and casseroles or grate the flesh into stir-fries.

Of all the brassicas, kohlrabi's the easiest to grow because, while snails occasionally take a chunk out of its tush, white cabbage butterfly caterpillars leave well alone – they simply trim the tops off.

Some people think it's bad luck to kill a butterfly and that 12 months of ill fortune will follow. Those people clearly don't grow cauliflowers – there's nothing worse than a cauliflower riddled with chubby green caterpillars. So I prefer to subscribe to Lincolnshire lore: anyone who crushes the first butterfly of the season will crush all their enemies that year. Here's hoping the aphids, whitefly, stinky green shield bugs, bronze beetles, mealybugs, slugs, snails and scale also take note.

Nocino liqueur

Quarter green walnuts and place in a large glass jar or ceramic crock with 6 whole cloves, 1 cinnamon stick, 2–3 star anise and the grated zest of 1 lemon and 1 orange. Add 1 litre cheap vodka and, if desired, a shot of espresso (a tip I got a few years ago from a self-sufficient Positano taxi driver named Enzo).

Store in a cool, dark cupboard and shake the jar every few days for at least a month, or until the walnuts disintegrate into a dark sludge. Strain through muslin and discard residue. Return vodka to the jar, add 500g caster sugar and shake daily for a fortnight. Strain again, then bottle.

Beetroot and mustard flowers

'Regal Red' cabbages

'Early Purple Vienna' kohlrabi

Clockwise from top: 'Rainbow Blend'; classic
'Majestic Red'; round 'Paris Market'; 'Solar Yellow'

Although not fully thornless, boysenberry 'Brûlée' is one of my favourites

DECEMBER 12: I've just picked the first kilogram of organic, spray-free – aka completely neglected – thornless boysenberries from our berry farm. They're sweet and juicy and full of extra protein from little looper caterpillars. (Though irritating in a bowl of fresh berries, these bugs are no bother when I'm making jam. As soon as the fruit simmers, they float to the surface and I scoop them out.)

When I first moved here, I had grand plans to turn our unused equestrian arena into a pick-your-own berry farm, but those grand plans have since been usurped by even grander plans for a formal French potager. That means the 150 thornless berry bushes I'd ordered – 50 each of 'Berry Delight' (a boysenberry/loganberry hybrid), 'Black Satin' blackberries and 'Thornless Jewel' boysenberries – have had to find other homes. Two dozen plants are now bedded into temporary trenches beside the driveway (along with 10 'Seckel' pears in the early stages of espalier training), there's another row in front of the chook run and the rest are planted between the apple trees in our orchard, with bee-friendly sweet alyssum, red clover and wild dog daisies at their feet. The romance of the scene, I should point out, is somewhat ruined by the ghastly black plastic netting I've flung over the rows to foil the birds. I must finish pegging it down. The dog managed to get stuck under it this week so there's a Border collie-sized hole somewhere.

WHEN I FIRST MOVED HERE, I HAD GRAND PLANS TO TURN OUR UNUSED EQUESTRIAN ARENA INTO A PICK-YOUR-OWN BERRY FARM

DECEMBER 13: Jason's insistence that I leave tidy tracts of bare earth between my rows of spuds and strawberries – just like his grandfather Fred used to do – has backfired wildly, and beautifully. As I haven't hoed or mulched or plucked a single self-sown seedling since spring, instead of wheelbarrow-wide access paths we've ended up with wheelbarrow-wide strips of weeds. Except all those tiny plants aren't weeds . . . but second generation silene, love-in-the-mist, blue cornflowers, gilia, gypsophila, corn poppies, linaria, alyssum and cosmos. My wildflower border is back!

For our wedding last summer, I sowed the 35-metre borders on each side of our lawn with Wildflower World's 'Lowfield Meadow' mix. It's a premium seed blend that behaves like a floral relay team, with the pastel shades of early spring passing the baton on to the reds and golds of late summer.

The seed packet promised that 'Lowfield Meadow' was quick to flower but, by this time last year, I'd started to have doubts. Six weeks out from our big day all there was to show for the bulk bag of seed I'd mixed with sand and painstakingly broadcast by hand was a faint green five o'clock shadow, so I shoved several thousand white cosmos into the mix too.

I needn't have panicked. Those wildflowers were spectacular (well at least the ones you could see through the forest of cosmos stalks), not just for our wedding but right up until they were cut down by the first frosts. In years to come, when I'm still yanking clumps of pink catchfly out of the corners of my plot, I may live to regret sowing wildflowers, but for now they're a pleasure rather than a pain.

DECEMBER 14: Disaster! Blight has ripped through my 'Beefsteak' tomato plants like a particularly juicy rumour. Tell-tale streaks of black are spreading up their stems, scarring the foliage and causing their heads to slump. I bundled all the infected plants into a black plastic rubbish bag but I fear I haven't acted quickly enough to save the 'Ilam Hardy' potatoes beside them.

Cornflowers

Cleome

Love-in-the-mist

Coreopsis

Cosmos

'Rainbow Blend'

'White Belgian'

DECEMBER 16: If I ever sow, dig or scrub another carrot in my life, it will be too soon. My 26 trial rows of carrots – every commercially available variety I could source – have spawned at least a thousand carrots. It took me and Jason three hours today to dig them up, relay them to the outdoor tap, wash the dirt from their tangerine (and, in some cases, purple, red, yellow and white) roots, and truss the carefully labelled bunches with twine so that Sally Tagg could photograph them all for *NZ Gardener*. It drizzled the whole time but Lucas, bless his six-month-old heart, didn't grizzle once. He slept through the entire ordeal.

Until today, I've never managed to pull off a skite-worthy crop of long, straight, crunchy carrots. You name it, I've encountered it: poor germination (or no germination), twisted and forked roots, vigorous tops with no bottoms and premature bolting. I was starting to take it personally, but it must simply be a numbers game. If at first you don't succeed, try again, en masse.

The pick of the crop? I'm rapt with 'Amsterdam Forcing' for long, slender carrots; the Kiwi classic 'Egmont Gold' for chunky, crunchy carrot sticks; gorgeous golden 'Lubyana'; the mighty hybrid 'Majestic Red' for all-round performance; lycopene-laden 'Nutri Red'; heirloom 'Purple Haze' (also sold as 'Purple Dragon', this variety dates back a thousand years, long before patriotic Dutch growers bred the orange carrots that are now the commercial norm); 'Solar Yellow' and the Flemish heirloom 'White Belgian', which is the spitting image of a botoxed parsnip. Some varieties – including 'Senior', which other growers swear is a winner – came a cropper when our cows got into the garden back in October; and, having sown them in alphabetical order, the varieties from T to Z got a raw deal at the far end of my trial bed (as the season has progressed, so has the shade cast by the oak tree on the corner of the lawn).

I've sent Sally home with a carload of carrots, Geoff's horses are happily munching through the forked and twisted rejects and I'll take the rest of my soon-to-be cover-star carrots to the farmers' market on Sunday.

DECEMBER 18: With up to 2000 seeds per packet – that's 50 roots for as little as 10c – carrots could well prove to be the most profitable crop I've ever sown. My tidy bunches with their perky green tops (they're edible too, if you have a taste for bitter greens) were quickly snapped up at the market this morning. The colourful types were most popular, so next spring I'll simply sow the 'Rainbow Blend' mix from Kings Seeds, which includes five vibrant varieties – 'Atomic Red', 'Bambino', 'Cosmic Purple', 'Lunar White' and 'Solar Yellow' – for the price of one.

DECEMBER 23: We're down to our last bucket of 'Jersey Benne' spuds. I sold the rest at the special twilight Christmas farmers' market in Clevedon this evening, along with bunches of 'Wiltshire Ripple' sweet peas, wee pots of plum jam and dozens of fresh raspberry and vanilla meringues. I need the yolks to make custard for my Christmas trifle, but Mum's on pavlova duty this year and I'd hate for all those whites to go to waste.

DECEMBER 25: We're having a self-sufficient Christmas dinner, with freshly dug 'Jersey Benne' potatoes, baby peas with mint, a rainbow of roasted baby carrots, a slow-roasted shoulder of lamb and the obligatory green salad (which, in our family, no one ever eats, so I'm thinking of tarting it up with festive red feijoa flowers – they're prettier than pohutukawa petals, and edible too).

And for dessert? Pavlova, cream puffs and two towering trifles – mine featuring sponges spread with boysenberry jam and soaked with Damson gin, a layer of tangy 'Berry Delight' hybrid berries smothered in a seven-egg custard and an obscene quantity of whipped cream, and my brother-in-law Alan's teetotaller version with raspberry jelly and tinned peaches.

It's amazing that anyone can afford to enjoy yuletide lamb, given the record prices being paid at the stock sales. They're going for well over $100 per head. (In Grandma's day, she had to hope for a mustering mishap to get her hands on prime lamb. From her diary, December 22, 1939: 'A lamb knocked itself out and Percy killed it, so now we have lamb for Christmas. Meanwhile the war drags on with nothing much happening, apart from ships and submarines sunk on both sides.')

Grandma's got one up on me. Our lamb, I must confess, came from the butcher in Pukekohe. Our bundles of joy are all still running around in the paddock. It just didn't seem terribly Christian to cut their throats for Christmas.

Feijoa flower

'Berry Delight' berries

Trifle

'Wiltshire Ripple' sweet peas

Boysenberry jam

DECEMBER 28: How I love the long lazy days between Christmas and the New Year, but what a sad, soggy excuse we've had for summer so far. We were supposed to go to the beach for a break but the weather forecast – how surprising – is for more miserable weather to come so we've stayed home.

Will summer ever arrive? I hope so. I'm adopting a better-late-than-never approach and have sown late crops of pumpkins, gherkins, cucumbers, two rows of colourful heirloom corn ('Rainbow Inca' and 'Hopi Blue'), five more rows of 'Dwarf Massey' peas and a packet of 'Fin de Bagnols' dwarf beans.

At least my dahlias are relishing all this rain. Last year Linda Brown from Dahlia Haven gave me a lucky dip selection of psychedelic single-flowered varieties as a wedding gift. These classic daisy-shaped dahlias are too plain for some but I much prefer them to the giant decorative and cactus types. Not only do they flower all summer long, they're a magnet for bedraggled bumblebees.

'Hopi Blue' corn

'Rainbow Inca' corn

My easy-care summer border of dahlias and zinnias

Dahlia 'Halo'

Species dahlias and unnamed seedlings from
Dahlia Haven's breeding programme

Field mushrooms

Dahlia 'Maltby Escort'

Sweet peas

Gladiolus 'Flevo Dancer'

'Sharon Anne' dahlias

Dahlia 'Barbara Kappler'

JANUARY 1: I've made a New Year's resolution. For the next twelve months, I've decided to keep a profit and loss account for my garden, to reveal exactly how much I spend on my favourite hobby – and to see if I can sell enough at the farmers' market to break even.

JANUARY 5: Lucas is shaping up to be my right-hand man in the garden. As I pull weeds, sow seeds and dead-head dahlias, my blond-haired, blue-eyed boy slips, slops, slaps and sits on the lawn. At six months, he's so easy to amuse. I let him pluck the petals off my echinaceas and Oriental poppies (at this rate, his first word won't be papa, but papaver) and play pass the parcel with 'Iceberg' lettuces. I've never seen anyone have so much fun tossing a salad.

I'm not a big fan of salads – give me a roast spud or a pile of buttery green beans any day – but I almost always have a patch of mesclun on the go. Rocket too, though the row I sowed in spring has long since bolted, spawning seedlings as thick as the hairs on a dog's back.

JANUARY 7: It has rained all day, again.

JANUARY 8: After all these wet days and warm nights, fungi are having a field day. In our far paddock, field mushrooms are cropping up around the crusty cow pats. I came across a cluster of immature buttons and flat-capped portobellos on our hill and spied an even bigger cluster on the neighbour's side of the boundary. If Jason hadn't been with me, I would have hurdled the fence and helped myself, but he'd die of embarrassment if we were ever caught in the act.

I didn't like mushrooms as a kid but I loved going foraging for them with Dad. We'd scoot around the paddocks before the cows could get in and trample them, my sister and I riding side-saddle on opposite sides of the quad bike. Mum always sliced them up to sauté in butter, but I prefer to roast the buttons whole with crushed garlic and olive oil and stuff the big portobellos with a mixture of Parmesan, breadcrumbs, garlic and cream.

I guess this early flush of fungi means we won't have any autumn mushrooms, but that's no big deal. I can buy a bag every week from Phil and Iona Matheson at the market instead.

JANUARY 12: It's raining again. We had a torrential downpour this morning that has ruined all the petals on my latest flush of roses. The rain would have ruined my 'Wiltshire Ripple' sweet peas too, had I not taken the secateurs to them last night. I picked 300 stems and have displayed them in a crate of old glass milk bottles.

It's often said that the best way to learn is by trial and error, and that's certainly proved true of my sweet peas. Not staking them has proved to be a blessing in disguise, for the vines have crawled across the asparagus bed, out of the shadow of the stables and into the sun. This could well be the perfect way to grow sweet peas for picking, as the flower stems are all long and straight – and easy to reach – whereas whenever I've trained these climbers up trellis or a tepee, they rapidly get to 2 metres before they even bother to bloom.

LUCAS IS SHAPING UP TO BE MY RIGHT-HAND MAN IN THE GARDEN

JANUARY 14: Hindsight is a beautiful thing, and so is the sight of 200 stately gladioli flowers all unfurling their flamboyant ruffled florets at once. I was pretty chuffed with myself for getting all the corms into the ground on a single frantic afternoon in October, but I really hadn't thought through the ramifications. You could set your calendar to a gladioli corm; they flower exactly 90 days after planting. If I'd staggered my crop, popping in a dozen corms a week, I could have enjoyed gorgeous gladdies right up until autumn. Instead they're all opening at once. If they don't sell at the market tomorrow, I'm afraid our house will end up looking like either a florist's shop or Dame Edna's boudoir.

To be honest, I may have overdone it with the pink dahlias this year too. They don't really go with our décor. I planted at least a dozen different varieties and they've all done well, especially 'Ruthie G'. This divine waterlily dahlia has pink blooms that seem to glow, thanks to a subtle touch of apricot in the centre. Despite only growing to about a metre, which means it doesn't need staking, it has elegant long stems for picking. The katydids like it too. They nip the tips off all its perfectly symmetrical petals. 'Bug man' Ruud Kleinpaste says I should collect them all up and feed them to my chooks, but I can't bring myself to do it. They might be vandals but katydids are almost cute – they look like short-legged, fat-bellied grasshoppers.

Dahlia 'Colt45'

Gladiolus 'Flevo Dancer'

Dahlia 'Tioga Lovesong'

Dahlia 'Jan Lennon'

JANUARY 15: The dahlias and gladdies, I'm glad to report, sold like hotcakes. I sold every stem, then blew my profits on a side of smoked salmon, two eye fillet steaks, a packet of organic pork spare ribs marinated in bourbon and brown sugar, a leg of lamb and 2.5kg of tomatoes (mine are failing to win the fight against blight so I have no choice but to buy them) – and I still had $64 in the till.

When I got home I logged onto the computer and immediately spent my spare change on mail-order seedlings from Awapuni Nurseries, specifically leeks, celeriac and two dozen blue delphiniums. Why delphiniums? Because blue flowers always sell first, and – aside from love-in-the-mist and hydrangeas, which are as common as muck in these parts – I've hardly got any left in my garden.

Taking a market stall has made me realise that my tastes don't always match those of my customers. The customer is always right I know, but I have to hold my tongue if people ask for yellow dahlias when I have perfectly good bunches of beautifully burgundy-splashed 'Blackberry Ripple' right under their noses.

THE DAHLIAS AND GLADDIES SOLD LIKE HOTCAKES

'Blackberry Ripple' dahlias

'Divinity' gladioli

gorgeous gladioli!
dahlias
beetroot swedes
red cabbages
globe artichokes
cavalo nero
yellow plums
carrots

Hydrangeas and love-in-the-mist

'Giant Red' mustard

BLUE
FLOWERS
ALWAYS
SELL FIRST,
AND I'VE
HARDLY GOT
ANY LEFT IN
MY GARDEN

JANUARY 16: It's shaping up to be a beaut season for beetroot (it's loving the rain) and burgers. A burger just isn't a burger without beetroot to stain the bun red. My favourite variety is 'Bull's Blood', not for its round ruby roots, but because it has the best-looking leaves. They're a ravishing dark red.

Mum always grew beets the size of swedes but mine never last that long in the garden. When they're 4 to 5cm in diameter, I steam my beets whole in the microwave, then slice the red flesh into fat wedges and toss, still warm, into rocket salads with soft goat's cheese. Steaming instead of boiling means they don't bleed any of their colour during the cooking process, so be prepared for bright pink urine the next morning.

JANUARY 17: I wasn't intending to make my own mustard when I sowed two rows of *Brassica juncea* 'Giant Red' in spring. I wasn't actually intending to eat it at all, aside from plucking the occasional peppery leaf to spice up my salads. I grow 'Giant Red' mustard purely as an ornamental – its metallic maroon foliage looks wicked in the garden – but it sets seed so readily that I figure I might as well use it. This is a dangerous game: mustard produces hundreds of seed pods that, when dry, split down the seams and fling their cargo quite a distance. I sense I'll be hoeing mustard seedlings out of my borders for years to come.

My plants started flowering in late November and all summer I've turned a blind eye to their garish golden blooms. Last week I cut the plants off at ground level, tied all the stalks together and bundled them, upside down, into black plastic rubbish bags inside the hothouse on our deck to fully dry.

I sorted the seed from the chaff this morning. It wasn't too laborious, though it did require three grades of sieve: a kitchen colander, an antique flour sifter and a fine mesh sieve to sift out the last bits of dust and debris.

'Giant Red' mustard

'Bull's Blood' beetroot

Preserved beetroot

To preserve beetroot for sandwiches and burgers, scrub but don't peel your beets. Bring to the boil in a large pot of water and simmer till tender; prod from time to time with a bamboo skewer to check their progress. Drain and set aside until they're just cool enough to handle, then turn on the cold tap and simply rub the skins off with your fingers before slicing and stacking into jars.

Make a pickling solution by combining 1 cup malt vinegar, ½ cup white sugar and 1 cup water. Bring to the boil, stirring until the sugar has dissolved, then pour over the sliced beetroot. Tap the sides of the jar with a knife to dislodge any air bubbles, then screw on airtight lids. It keeps for up to 12 months.

Red mustard seeds

English mustard

Yellow mustard seeds (the best variety for seeds is 'Salad White' from Kings Seeds) are far bigger than black or brown seeds, which makes them easier to pummel in a mortar and pestle or blitz in a food processor to make mustard powder. I initially tried to use a whizz stick in a tall jar but it wasn't tall enough to stop a whirlwind of mustard seeds spraying out all over the kitchen. Once you've got mustard powder, just mix it with cold water for instant hot mustard, like classic Colman's English.

Beer and honey mustard

I use my own hop beer to make this wholegrain mustard, though any ale will do. Soak 100g yellow mustard seeds and 100g black or brown mustard seeds overnight in 1 cup beer. Set aside half the soaked seeds and purée the rest with 100ml runny honey, 2 tablespoons good quality olive oil, 1 tablespoon white vinegar and 1 teaspoon salt. Scrape out of blender into a bowl and stir in reserved whole seeds. Add finely chopped or minced herbs – try thyme and rosemary – or a deseeded chilli and citrus peel.

Homemade hotdog mustard

This mild American mustard gets its golden glow from ground turmeric.

In a small glass bowl, soak ½ cup yellow mustard seeds in 1 cup water and 100ml white vinegar overnight. Purée in a blender or food processor until smooth (add extra water if required). Place in a small pot with ½ teaspoon salt, a pinch of garlic powder, a pinch of paprika and 1 teaspoon ground turmeric. Bring to the boil, whisking constantly, then reduce heat and simmer for a few minutes, until thick. Store in the fridge.

JANUARY 20: I won't make it to the market this weekend – we're going to the beach instead – so this morning I packed a crate of fresh cut flowers and took them to work to flog to my publishing colleagues. I made $54.50 selling dahlias, gladioli and hand-tied tussie-mussies, but instead of prudently pocketing the proceeds, I spent them on two bottles of bubbles, a bar of chocolate and bags of chips for Friday night drinks with the *NZ Gardener* team. Three weeks into the new year, I don't hold much hope that my gardening endeavours will prove profitable.

JANUARY 23: It hasn't rained all week, and that's the first time I can say that this summer. I'm glad to finally see the sun because most of our golden plums split in the rain and I'd hate to see the same fate befall our red plum tree.

When I moved to Hunua, the only fruit trees on the property were a miserable 'Meyer' lemon and two lichen-clad plum trees that produced about half a dozen fruit each. But last summer we cut down the old conifer shelterbelt that was shading them and suddenly they've got a new lease on life. I'm not sure whether it's due to the extra sunlight, or because I've improved their pollination hit rate by planting 15 new plums around the existing trees, but they're going great guns now. I've already picked 10kg of yellow plums (I bottled some, sold some and froze the rest) and the red plum is absolutely laden. It's so laden that its branches are now dragging on the ground, which made it a bit tricky when I attempted to wrap bird netting around them tonight.

I'VE ALREADY PICKED 10KG OF YELLOW PLUMS AND THE RED PLUM IS ABSOLUTELY LADEN

Ripening 'Satsuma' plums

Early fruiting 'Shiro' plums

JANUARY 24: I've just received an illuminating email from my neighbour Greg. He heard me gloating on the radio about my corker crop of plums. 'Do you think,' he asked wryly, 'that the fact that your neighbours have got 250,000 new bees could have something to do with it?'

Indeed it might. It might also explain why I heard all those honey bees buzzing in our cherry trees back in spring. Given that the varroa mite has wiped out New Zealand's colonies of wild bees, it should have occurred to me sooner that they must have come from a neighbourly hive.

I've told Greg his bees are welcome to feast on my flowers any day, and I'll happily help him eat his honey. (Technically they're Greg's wife Michelle's bees. One of the reasons she moved to the country was to keep bees. She lovingly handpainted their hives, only to discover that she's allergic to her charges.)

I'm keen to get my own bees. When I was a child we were never short of honey. A local beekeeper kept his hives on our farm and paid us with a tray of raw honeycomb and several litres of spun clover honey each season. My grandparents kept bees ('After tea Percy tackled the bees,' Grandma wrote in her diary, 'and he got a good deal of both honey and stings') and so did my Uncle John. When a wild swarm took up residence behind our cowshed one spring, Uncle John came to collect them. When he turned up at the farm in a shirt, shorts and gumboots, we thought nothing of it. He was a bee whisperer, even if Dad thought he was mad.

We stood well back and watched as Uncle John attempted to coax that angry swarm into a large box. All seemed to be going to plan until Uncle John suddenly developed a worried look on his face, dropped his pants and made a panicked run for the cowshed. Dad had to blast all the bees off him with the high pressure hose we used to clean the muck out of the yard.

Michelle's decorated beehives

JANUARY 28: I used to judge a good summer by the singlet strap marks on my shoulders and the pallid jandals stencilled on my feet by the sun, but this summer I haven't even had to get the sunscreen out. Our hay paddock has been locked up for eight weeks and the grass is now a knee-high haze of pale gold, the same shade my hair used to turn after 10 days at Hot Water Beach as a kid. When I walk through it, black field crickets leap out of the long grass like an infestation of fleas in shabby carpet.

It really should have been baled by now. Good hay has an aroma as sweet as molasses, while bad hay smells like deceased estate sales. Leave it uncut for too long and it loses its vitality and ends up full of weed seeds, but bale it too soon and it can be a fire hazard. Stacks of green bales heat up like a green compost heap – they've been known to occasionally self-combust

and burn rural barns down.

I haven't helped make hay in 20 years but I can still recall every step of the process. First, Dad would consult the long-range forecast. Second, Dad would ignore the long-range forecast. He'd cut the grass one day, turn it for two, then whisk it into windrows – like the soft peak stage of a meringue – on the fourth. Leonard Irving always baled it and Dad's mate Neal Phillips always picked it up in his blue-green truck.

Dad and Neal worked well together. Neal drove (quietly) while Dad (not so quietly) barked orders at all of us – my cousins, nextdoor neighbours, any agriculture students from Lincoln University who happened to be seeking work experience in the district, and my sister and me. It was our job to run ahead of the truck, lining up the bales like golden dominoes so they'd feed neatly up the escalator to be stacked.

avolo nero

Meanwhile Mum milked the cows, put the beer on ice and made endless rounds of pikelets and toasted sandwiches. All going well, we'd get the last load into the barn just as it got dark on the night before we were due to depart for the beach.

There'll be no such palaver here today. We're only baling one paddock and Jason can stack the lot on the quad bike trailer, so there's no need for me to make pikelets.

JANUARY 29: My cavolo nero has been stunning this summer so, naturally, no one would buy any of it at the market today. I resorted to name-dropping to drum up business. 'Sophie Grigson,' I told my customers, 'sautés onion, thinly sliced fresh chilli, garlic and sprigs of fresh rosemary in a pan then tosses chopped cavolo nero on top and gently cooks it till tender.' 'Who's Sophie Grigson?' they replied. 'Have you heard of the Hairy Bikers?' I'd counter. (I watch far too much Food TV). 'They sauté shredded cavolo nero with butternut squash, garlic, Swiss chard, toasted pine nuts and lemon zest then cram it into crêpes smothered in cheese fondue.'

None of it worked. With a basket of cavolo nero and bugger all else left to sell, I was whipping together a bouquet of pointy white 'Snowflake' hydrangeas and purple anemones when my last customer, a lady named Fenella, ever-so-politely asked for a few cavolo nero leaves in her bouquet too.

Alison's cavolo nero and ham tart

When *NZ Gardener* food writer Alison Worth and her husband Burton sell kale at the Hamilton Farmers' Market, they offer free recipes to convince cagey customers. Serve this tart sliced or rolled up with salad leaves for a picnic treat.

Method: Chop 5 to 6 kale leaves and finely dice 1 small onion. Sauté in olive oil until soft, then spread over 2 sheets of puff pastry. Mix 2 eggs with 100g crème fraîche and spread over the pastry. Top with torn slices of shaved champagne ham, sprinkle with 100g grated Gruyère or Parmesan and season with sea salt and freshly ground black pepper. Bake at 200°C until golden brown. Garnish with Italian flat leaf parsley or oregano and serve warm.

Blackberry jelly

Wild blackberry jelly

Roughly chop 3 large cooking apples (peel, cores and all) and place in a pot with just enough water to cover. Bring to the boil, pop the lid on and simmer for 10 minutes, until the flesh is soft. Stir in 1kg blackberries and simmer for 10 minutes then lightly mash the fruit with a potato masher. Pour into a jelly bag and let drip overnight. (If you don't have a jelly bag, use a sieve lined with muslin or a cheap pillowcase. I once confessed in my *Sunday* column to using a pair of footless Glassons tights, tied off at the ankles, which so horrified then-CEO of Fairfax, Joan Withers, that she bought me a proper cloth bag.) Never squeeze your jelly bag to eke out every last drop of juice; this can turn the jelly cloudy. Measure the volume of juice and add an equal amount of sugar. Bring to the boil, stirring until the sugar has dissolved, then boil hard for 10 to 15 minutes until setting point is reached. Use a wooden spoon to scoop off any scum that forms. Pour jelly into warm, sterilised glass jars and seal.

'Black Satin'

I CAN'T IMAGINE LIVING IN THE COUNTRY WITHOUT BEING ABLE TO FORAGE FOR BLACKBERRIES

JANUARY 30: Ask any country gardener for their top maintenance tip and I bet they'll tell you that 'the best way to weed is with Roundup'. I don't like spraying weeds with herbicides and my city garden was proudly spray-free (though I did dole out the odd box of slug bait), but now that I live in the country, I have to take a more pragmatic approach. Take our leafy liquidambar-lined driveway: it's more than 100 metres long. Weeding it by hand would be like painting the Sydney Harbour Bridge – as soon as it was finished, I'd have to start all over again.

My vegetable garden and orchard are 100 per cent spray-free, but the paths down the hill, the driveway and paddocks are Jason's domain and he's enlisted Dad to tackle the wild blackberries with Conquest.

I must admit to a twinge of regret. As a kid, I loved going foraging for wild blackberries along the roadsides, but it's a bit different when the jolly things go foraging in return. Not only do these prickly thugs try to grab my ankles, they snare our unshorn sheep and pull at Mr Puppy

Doo-Hawg's long hair. Not content to colonise our gullies, wild blackberry brambles have now infiltrated the flax bank below the equestrian arena and, at the rate they're climbing the hill, I'll be able to pick blackberries out of my hornbeam hedge next summer.

I can't imagine living in the country without being able to forage for blackberries, so I've planted the well-behaved thornless variety 'Black Satin'. It lacks the ferocious vigour of its feral cousin – my first crop is fairly pitiful – but I've picked just enough to make a small jar of blackberry jelly for Mum. Her favourite childhood dessert was rice pudding with fresh cream and a scoop of Grandma Clarice's tangy blackberry jelly on top.

JANUARY 31: Lucas has been helping me and Mum bottle red plums. He's our official quality control officer. He takes the fruit out of the jars almost as fast as we can slice and stack it in, and faithfully samples the flesh. When we open the jars in winter, I shudder to think how many of those plums will bear baby bite marks.

We've made 10 jars of jam, bottled a dozen large jars of halved plums – that's two batches in my vintage Agee waterbath preserver – and another dozen of stewed pulp using the overflow method. Though less satisfying from an aesthetic perspective (jars of pulp aren't nearly as pretty on the shelf), the overflow method is far easier. Simply pour piping hot fruit into warm Agee jars, slide on a lid, screw on the bands and flip them on their heads to seal. That's the theory, anyway. Instead of warming the jars, I accidentally cranked the oven up too high, causing the first two jars to explode when the hot fruit hit the glass. It made a hell of mess.

We got through one basket of fruit before calling it quits. There's a plum sponge pudding in the oven now and I'll freeze the rest to make plum sauce and spicy chutney.

'Satsuma' plums

Spicy plum chutney

If I could grow dates, sweet date chutney would be my favourite homemade condiment to serve with cheese and crusty bread. As I can't, plum chutney has to do. I make a batch of this at the same time as I make plum sauce each summer, as the ingredients are fairly similar and both make our tiny house pong of vinegar.

Method: Halve and stone 1kg red plums. Place in a large pot with 2 roughly chopped cooking apples, 2 diced onions, 600ml cider vinegar, 500g brown sugar, 1 tablespoon crushed garlic, 1 fresh red cayenne pepper, 2 teaspoons ground ginger and 1 teaspoon each of sea salt, black pepper, ground cinnamon, ground allspice and ground cloves. Bring to the boil, stirring until the sugar has dissolved. Reduce heat and simmer for at least 1 hour, stirring occasionally to prevent sticking, until the chutney thickens. Pour into hot, sterilised glass jars and seal. Store for at least 1 month to allow the flavours to develop before opening.

Granddad Evan's plum sauce

My Granddad was no gourmand. He loathed yoghurt and poncy modern mesclun salads with vinaigrette. His definition of a salad was shredded 'Iceberg' with mayonnaise made from a tin of sweetened condensed milk, a teaspoon of mustard powder and a tablespoon of malt vinegar – and the only other sauce to pass his lips was plum sauce. There was always a bottle of it on my grandparents' dining table.

Method: Rinse, halve and stone 2.5kg firm red plums. Place in a large pot with 1 litre malt vinegar, 1kg sugar, 2 diced onions, 1 tablespoon crushed garlic, a grated knob of fresh ginger, 1 tablespoon salt, 1 teaspoon fresh chilli, 2 teaspoons ground cloves and 2 teaspoons cracked black peppercorns. Bring to the boil, stirring until the sugar has dissolved, then simmer over a low heat for an hour. Take off the heat, purée smooth, pour into bottles and seal.

Bottled plums

'Black Hungarian' peppers

'Fin de Bagnols' beans

'Cabernet' peppers

'Pinocchio's Nose' chillis

'Rainbow Lights' silverbeet

FEBRUARY 1: Jason isn't keen on spicy food but I think it's time his taste buds toughened up. I've been picking pecks of peppers – from spicy habaneros and Scotch bonnets to fiery 'Serrano' chillies – and someone has to eat them.

Chillis are a doddle to grow but I've always struggled to grow decent bell peppers like the glasshouse-grown capsicums sold in the shops. Mine are invariably small and thin-walled, even if I lavish them with liquid fertiliser and install a well-placed sprinkler to quench their thirst. I've had success this year with the sweet pepper 'Cabernet' and the Italian heirloom 'Cornos Red', which is shaped like a bull's horn, though I can't claim any credit. I acquired the plants from a wholesale nursery in Whenuapai and they came with the fruit already on them.

I really didn't need to grow any chillis this year – I had such a bumper crop of cayenne peppers last summer that I'm still working through the jar of dried chilli in my pantry – but I couldn't resist flinging in half a dozen intriguing varieties. I liked the sound of 'Pinocchio's Nose' and the quirky Bishop's hat shape of 'Habanero Flyer', which happens to be my favourite variety for sweet chilli sauce. For hot chilli sauce, I also put in a row of 'Serrano', a chubby chilli that's fleshier than a cayenne pepper, with a torpedo shape.

In spring, Mandy Villacorte from Mandeville Gardens in Onewhero gave me a dozen 'Black Hungarian' seedlings at the farmers' market and their fruit has been the first to ripen. 'Black Hungarian' was introduced by Kings Seeds a few summers ago but it no longer features in their catalogue. Mandy saves her own seed, and I'm pleased she does, because the plant's a beauty, with dark purple veins and stems, lilac flowers and liquorice-black, bullet-shaped fruit as shiny as miniature eggplants. The flavour's mild but when these peppers fully ripen to red they develop more of a hit, though it's still a gentle nip rather than a vicious bite.

'Pinocchio's Nose', however, has proved to be a piranha by comparison. Not only are these chillis huge – up to 25cm long – they're insanely hot. If only I'd read the label (the Thompson and Morgan seed catalogue describes them as 'almost atomic') before I chopped my crop into a 9-litre pot of homemade pasta sauce . . . without wearing kitchen gloves. My hands are now burning and my tongue is too. Even after diluting it with four large tins of tomatoes, that sauce is too spicy to eat. I sent a tub of it home with Lucas's babysitter Melissa – her flatmates aren't afraid of hot food – and used the rest to make a huge batch of chilli con carne with dried borlotti beans, diced carrots and finely sliced 'Fin de Bagnols' beans. A dozen tubs of it are now packed neatly into the chest freezer. Poor Jason doesn't know what he's in for.

FEBRUARY 2: My fingers are still on fire. Despite rubbing them with the gooey sap of a split aloe vera leaf, the burn doesn't seem to be easing – and I still can't feel the tip of my tongue.

FEBRUARY 3: Rambo is an unlikely ladykiller but his lovemaking has just bolstered our bank account by $1514.15. We've sent all but one of our lambs to the sales (the sole survivor needs treatment for fly strike). Dairy cows bellow for days when their babies are taken off them but our sheep didn't even seem to notice, though perhaps that's because I distracted them with a fresh paddock.

FEBRUARY 5: If I squint, I can almost imagine I'm in Central Otago. The cows might have sabotaged my vision of a hillside thick with colourful Russell lupins, like the wild ones on South Island postcards, but I came home from the farmers' market today with a 6kg crate of Cromwell apricots.

A savvy Central Otago orchardist has cottoned on to the fact that stone-fruit-starved Aucklanders will pay almost anything for fresh, flavoursome apricots . . . because we can't grow our own. Apricot trees that crop well in warmer climates are the stuff of legend. Everyone seems to know someone whose grandma or great aunt had an abundant apricot tree in the central city when they were a child, but they're all a little vague if I ask for exact GPS coordinates.

My ex-boyfriend had a good apricot tree in his Auckland garden, and by good I mean that it once excelled itself and produced 17 fruit. I pinched them all for a photo shoot, then ate the evidence.

When I bought my house in Western Springs, it had an old overgrown apricot tree on the front boundary. I pruned it carefully and was rewarded with the princely sum of three apricots the following summer, and none the year after that. The third year, I chopped it down and put a 'Granny Smith' apple in its place.

I've planted 'Tomcot' and 'Sundrop' apricot trees here but I don't hold much hope of ever getting a crop.

It defies my locavore logic to buy apricots that have been driven from one end of the country to the other, but my eco-standards allow for a little flexibility. The way I look at it, it's far better for the planet for me to purchase fresh apricots with a few food miles under their belts than bland canned apricots shipped here from South Africa. Ever since the Roxdale apricot factory shut down a few years ago, it hasn't been possible to buy New Zealand-grown canned apricots – so I figure I'll just bottle my own. I filled 14 large Agee jars with halved apricots and another six with sliced, stewed fruit then, in a stroke of culinary genius, churned the leftover stewing syrup in my ice cream machine to make a sensational sorbet.

FEBRUARY 7: The Clevedon Garden Circle is coming for a summer picnic next week. It'll probably rain – all it has done this summer is rain – so I've bought a cheap portable white canvas pergola. Mum's coming over today to pimp it up with some of our wedding bunting. Though I own a sewing machine, I haven't yet learned how to thread it.

Hybrid Russell lupins

'Moorpark' apricots

'Damson' plums

FEBRUARY 10: Our kitchen looks like the set of a splatter film. There's plum jam stuck to every surface. I picked a basketful of 'Damson' plums – also known as the plum of Damascus – from the trees in the chook run today. Though too tart to eat fresh (even for lovers of sour lollies), these marble-sized plums with their dusty indigo skins are my favourites for jam – indeed they're the only plum I use.

On the dairy farm where I grew up, there were two 'Damson' trees in the orchard by the cowshed. They cropped so prolifically that our pantry was never short of plum jam. We ate it on toast for breakfast and were packed off to school with plum jam sandwiches for lunch (occasionally we'd get pickled onion and cheese, which was markedly more valuable for schoolyard bartering).

There's nothing my mum can't do with a jar of jam: we ate jammy steamed puddings, red rainbow-like sponge rolls and latticed tarts that looked like stained glass windows when they came out of the oven. And whenever Mum made shepherd's pie for dinner, she'd trim the puff pastry off the corners of the pie dish, spread the scraps thickly with jam and pop them into the oven for pudding.

When making jam, I simply bring plums to the boil with a little water to stop them sticking, squash lightly with a wooden spoon or potato

Damson gin

Wash and pat dry enough 'Damson' plums to fill a 2-litre glass jar or food-grade plastic container. Prick each plum with a kebab stick and pack tightly into the container, sprinkling with 1–2 cups of sugar. Pour in a bottle of cheap gin. Shake the container every few days until the sugar has dissolved, then store in a cool, dark cupboard for at least three months. Strain (serve the sozzled plums with ice cream) and bottle.

masher, then shove in an equal quantity of sugar and stir until the sugar has dissolved. Boil it hard for 5–10 minutes, scoop out the stones as they rise to the surface, skim off the scum, pour into jars and seal. Because plums are rich in pectin, I've never had a batch fail to set.

Even better than 'Damson' jam is 'Damson' gin. I make this liqueur every year so that, come Christmas, I can soak my trifle sponge in it instead of brandy or sherry. It's delicious and dead easy to make – the only hard part is not quaffing the lot before December.

FEBRUARY 11: This summer I've underestimated how easy it is to grow 'Regal Red' cabbages and overestimated their market appeal. I have four dozen mature cabbages in my garden and no hope of shifting them all before they split out of their skins and bolt to seed. In desperation, I talked them up on Paul Holmes's Saturday morning radio show on Newstalk ZB today, then casually mentioned that I'll be selling them at the Clevedon Farmers' Market tomorrow.

FEBRUARY 12: This morning I witnessed the awesome power of harnessing someone else's celebrity. My cabbages all sold before 10 a.m. I spent the proceeds on French crêpes, another crate of apricots and a fat spaghetti squash from my neighbours Jim and Rae Heatley at Dullumbunda Farm in the Hunua hills. (Spaghetti squash are so-named because, once cooked, their flesh is easily shredded into noodle-like strands.)

Red Regal' cabbages

Spaghetti squash

'Printanor' garlic

FEBRUARY 13: Garlic is traditionally planted on the shortest day in winter and harvested on the longest in summer but I'm running late this year. I've pulled 86 perfect piquant bulbs so far but I suspect there are still a few more buried behind the stables. Having left them in the ground far too long, some of the tops have died down and rotted off.

I shared my garlic growing pleasure – and frustration – in my *Sunday Star-Times* column yesterday. I wrote that my garlic bulbs were a joy to behold, and how easy it would be to joyously behold them if only I was capable of braiding the stalks into a big fat French plait.

I blame my mother. While my primary school friends graduated from pigtails to fancy French plaits, Mum's hairdressing expertise extended to a pudding bowl and a sharp pair of scissors. She never plaited our hair. I tried to teach myself how to braid by watching hairdressing how-to videos on YouTube. (Unlike a simple three-strand plait, the French plait starts at the crown and gradually weaves in sections from the sides to create a symmetrical braid to the nape of the neck.)

How hard can it be to braid garlic? I tugged and tied and held the bulbs down with my toes, but it was a lost cause. My braid was lopsided and loose. When I held it up to admire, it immediately unwound in my hands. In the end I settled for simple Pippi Longstocking plaits.

Within hours of the Sunday paper hitting the newsstand, several readers – none of whom appear to be hairdressers – had emailed garlic braiding instructions. Robyn Toomath from Waiheke Island told me that her husband did a fabulous job plaiting her garlic crop, having never plaited anything in his life before. She suggested I refine my internet search terms. 'He went to YouTube, searched for "plaiting garlic" and followed the video slavishly.'

Mission Bay pharmacist Peter Balle says his 83-year-old dad grows mighty fine garlic (he sells it in his shop, along with homegrown 'Beefsteak' tomatoes). 'He'd plait three bulbs together to sell at his gate and I thought there had to be a better, more attractive way. I found a number of YouTube videos and website diagrams and managed to produce a decent example for my own kitchen. However, you need very strong hands – preferably three or four – and it would probably be easier once the stalks have dried a bit and are not so thick.'

'I'm sure you'll be inundated with people sending you easy instructions for braiding garlic,' added Barbara Olsen-Henderson, 'but I won't let that put me off.' She ordered me to 'undo your Pippi Longstocking plaits' and, in no fewer than 730 words, she spelled out exactly how to braid garlic. 'It's easy,' Barbara concluded. 'Actually it's not easy but it is possible. And when you're finished, you will feel intensely satisfied and proud of yourself and you'll need to phone a few people to come and admire it. I know this from experience.'

Sadly, I've proved Barbara wrong. I still can't braid and instead of feeling proud and satisfied, I just feel intensely jealous. Not only had she sent me detailed instructions, Barbara had sent photos of her own perfect braids.

At least I won't lose any sleep trying to braid my elephant garlic. I haven't grown enough to plait. The charming white 'Snowland' chrysanthemum daisies I put in to keep it company outgrew their welcome and smothered it. Of the 16 cloves I planted, I reaped four miserable bulbs. I'd have been better off just eating the seed.

> I'VE PULLED 86 PERFECT PIQUANT BULBS SO FAR BUT I SUSPECT THERE ARE STILL A FEW MORE BURIED BEHIND THE STABLES

FEBRUARY 14: I'm officially in panic mode. The Clevedon Garden Circle is coming to visit tomorrow. (I'm sure I wouldn't be worrying half as much if it was just called the Clevedon Garden Club, but somehow 'circle' makes it sound so much more official. I'm half expecting the ladies to turn up in floral hats with matching handbags and posh packed lunches of cucumber sarnies and tiny squares of Louise cake.)

What was I thinking when I agreed to let them visit in late summer? I certainly wasn't thinking about all the work that needed doing. I've indulged in a fair bit of instant gardening – strategically shoving large flowering plants from the garden centre into any gaps – and Nicola has spent two days this week weeding, while Jason has dutifully spread a truckload (actually two) of black mulch. What a difference it makes! It's like sweeping all the dust under the carpet.

When Jason's finished mulching, he's heading back to Bunnings on an emergency pergola purchasing mission. How lovely ours looked last night, rigged up in the middle of the neatly mown lawn with its green floral flags flapping in the breeze. It was a somewhat sorrier sight this morning though. When the wind rose last night, so did the pergola: it lifted right off the ground and broke all the legs off its metal frame.

FEBRUARY 15: They came, they saw, they complimented. The sun shone, the tea flowed – and there wasn't a cucumber sandwich in sight. It was a splendid day all round, though Jason was mortified when he came home three hours later to find me taking the ladies on a tour down the weedy hill, around the weedy equestrian arena, up the path past the weedy asparagus bed, past the weedy chicken run to our unmown orchard. 'You were only supposed to show them the best bits,' he sighed.

'White Emergo' runner beans

JASON AND I HAVE ALREADY SLIPPED INTO TRADITIONAL GENDER ROLES: 'IM OUTDOORS AND 'ER INDOORS

FEBRUARY 19: Husbands are like horses. You have to break them in at a young age ('while they can still be trained', according to Mum and my mother-in-law Maureen). My domestic mentors have been married for more than 40 years to husbands who, though undeniably handy when it comes to matters mechanical, both reckon cleaning and cooking is women's work. (I'm not exaggerating. When we took Mum out on a girls' night, Dad rang my brother-in-law to find out whether he should take the plastic wrap off a frozen pizza before bunging it into the oven.)

Twelve months down the track, I better start cracking my spousal whip because Jason and I have already slipped into traditional gender roles: 'im outdoors and 'er indoors. He mows the lawn, services the car and assembles anything requiring an Allen key, while I do the washing, (occasionally) dust and clean and always seem to end up doing the dishes. (It reminds me of the retro tea towel Heather from Mapua Country Trading sent as a wedding gift. This reads, 'It starts when you sink in his arms and ends with your arms in the sink'.)

Speaking of wedding presents, we've just taken possession of a pair of exquisite ceramic vessels from Nelson artist Katie Gold. I've always loved Katie's work and these colourful sculptures were commissioned as a wedding gift from my magazine colleagues. I've slipped them into the garden between the strawberries and summer phlox.

Beki's crispy pig's ear salad

You can't turn a sow's ear into a silk purse, but Sunday Painters' chef Beki Lamb turns little piggy lugs into a surprisingly scrumptious salad. I'm not usually one for ordering offal and animal extremities but I was intrigued by the combination of crunchy apple, curly endive and crispy pig.

Method: In a large pot, cover 6 pig's ears with water and add a carrot, onion, celery stalk, fennel bulb, bay leaf and sage. Simmer on low for 6 hours or until very tender. Carefully remove from stock and lay flat in a single layer on a tray lined with baking paper. Set aside to cool, then refrigerate overnight. Slice pig's ears thinly and deep fry in vegetable oil until crispy – watch out as the oil may spit. Serve immediately, tossed through shredded curly endive (or finely chopped witlof) and julienned 'Granny Smith' apple with a soubise dressing. To make the dressing, sauté 500g diced onion in 100g butter until soft, then add a peeled, cored and diced 'Granny Smith' apple. Cook gently for 10 minutes, then purée and stir in 1 teaspoon wholegrain mustard, a squeeze of lemon juice and season to taste with salt and pepper.

At least I didn't have to cook or do the dishes tonight. Jason took me out to dinner, to Sunday Painters in Auckland's Ponsonby Road. It's one of my favourite restaurants – how I wish I had a dining room to decorate with a charming bistro theme! – so we could celebrate our anniversary with French champagne and crispy pig's ears.

eramic vessels by Nelson artist Katie Gold

'California Early Turban' garlic

FEBRUARY 24: Two years ago, I received an email from Dallas Curtis, convenor of the produce section at the Kaikoura A&P Show, enquiring of my availability to judge at the 100th anniversary show this year. I usually can't say what I'm doing next week, let alone the year after next, so naturally I agreed. I can't resist an A&P Show, especially a centennial one where everyone's promising to turn up in top hats and tails or corsets and buxom bustles.

This morning I left Jason holding the baby while my friend Rachel and I flew to Christchurch, picked up a rental car and set off on a girls' road trip up the coast to Kaikoura. We're flying home from Nelson and we plan to stop at every antique store and winery along the way.

At The White Cat Emporium in Cheviot, I bought three of the biggest garlic bulbs I've ever seen. They were grown by an organic gardener in nearby Gore Bay. I'll eat half the cloves and save the rest to plant next winter.

FEBRUARY 25: I woke up this morning suffering from a profound sense of guilt. Rachel and I have been put up, literally, in plush luxury at the Hapuku Treehouses. Our room in the lodge is bigger than my house, and far classier. While Jason and Lucas were at home eating porridge for breakfast, I was enjoying a duck confit hash cooked by Fiona Read. (A contestant on season two of *Masterchef*, she was undone by a batch of fudge truffles shaped into sports balls.)

It's just as well we ate a hearty breakfast because eyeing up the entries in the A&P Show's cookery competition was enough to make anyone's mouth water. All the classics were represented, from jam-filled sponge rolls to perfect pikelets, neenish tarts, butterfly cakes and station brownies. I'd never heard of a station brownie before, but apparently this cross between a sultana cake and a fruit loaf is a high country classic.

In the cut flower category, I admired row upon row of velvety red 'Loving Memory' exhibition-grade roses and ogled Graham Wilson's prize-winning Premier Dahlia – a bloom as big as an infant's noggin – before getting to work judging the vegetables.

I don't know what local crayfisherman Paul Reinke feeds his spuds but you'd only need to dig one for dinner, and Brian Arthur's red onions were the size of small watermelons. I caused a minor controversy in Class 180: 'Any unusual vegetable'. Some wag had attached fins and a flipper to a whale of a zucchini, entering it as an orcini. I awarded it first prize, prompting consternation from the owner of some comely chicory.

I judged the outdoor exhibits with the local MP, Colin King. We gave the Best in Show sash to Graham Calvert of the NZ Vintage Machinery Club, then – my official duties done – Rachel, Dallas and I sat on hay bales, eating hotdogs and watching a heading dog herd ducks. They say you can't teach an old dog new tricks but I couldn't help but wonder whether Mr Puppy Doo-Hawg could be similarly schooled with our Pekin ducks.

Barry's elderberry wine

In the Home Industries section at the Kaikoura A&P Show, retired schoolteacher Barry Dunnett won best plonk with his elderberry wine. Having made some unsavoury elderberry tipples in my time (when I asked a *Cuisine* staffer to suggest a suitable match for my 2008 vintage, they said 'your worst enemy'), I hit him up for his recipe.

He quoted from H E Bravery's 1958 book *Home Wine Making Without Failures*. For a rich, port-style, full-bodied wine, crush 3lb (1.4kg) elderberries, cover with 1 gallon (4.5 litres) water and soak overnight. Strain and boil juice for 5 minutes. Add 4lb (1.8kg) sugar to a fermenting vessel and pour over hot liquid. Let cool then stir in 1oz (28g) yeast. Cover and stand for 14 days before bottling.

No sooner had I finished converting the ingredients than Barry added, 'I don't stick to the recipe, of course.' He shovels 10kg of wild Central Otago elderberries into his wife Jenny's jelly bag, flings it into a plastic barrel with enough water to cover, then lets it steep for a few days. Squeeze and strain, bring to the boil (this kills rogue wild yeasts), add 5kg sugar and top up to 20 litres. Barry doesn't bother with fancy French wine yeast either. He just biffs in a tablespoon of dried breadmaker's yeast, gives it a good stir and siphons it off a year later.

A&P Show station brownie

This is the recipe supplied to entrants in Class 204 of the cookery section. In 2011, the first prize rosette went to Dot Halliday.

In a saucepan, simmer 2 cups sugar, 2½ cups water, 250g mixed fruit, ¼ teaspoon salt and 2 tablespoons butter for 5 minutes, then take off heat and stir in 1 heaped teaspoon of baking soda. When cool, fold in 3 cups flour, 1 teaspoon baking powder, 1 teaspoon cinnamon and ½ teaspoon mixed spice. Bake in a greased, lined loaf tin for 1½ hours at 150°C.

Elderberries

My Pekin ducks

FEBRUARY 27: Something's rotten in our stables. When I walked past this morning on the way to feed the chooks, I detected a distinct whiff of something rather rank emanating out of the end bay. It turns out that, sometime earlier this month, my darling husband had accidentally unplugged the chest freezer, spoiling its contents. I chucked the thawed golden plums to the chooks; the dogs can have a big bowl of festering chilli con carne for dinner.

FEBRUARY 28: When Jason got out of bed this morning, he looked out of the upstairs window and announced, 'It's foggy on Foggydale Farm.' I knew the name would grow on him.

FEBRUARY 29: An extra day in summer is usually a good thing, but this summer has been such a dud that I'll be glad to see the back of it. Our tank has only run dry a couple of times, which is a blessing I suppose, but we've barely seen any sun. My eggplants haven't flowered, my heritage corn's only knee-high and all my tomatoes have now succumbed to blight.

My late summer flower garden, at least, is a joy, though I'm puzzled how – given my lack of love for the colour yellow – I've somehow woven an autumnal tapestry of gold, citron, tangerine and peach. I can't turn down free plants, which explains all the clumps of shaggy apricot dahlias (my mum's golfing mate Judy gave me a bucket of tubers before our wedding), but how was I to know that the mixed punnets of dwarf zinnias I slipped in would all turn out to be either yellow or orange?

In my hot border, there are sunflowers streaked with bronze – the 'Petite Bouquet' mix from Kings Seeds – and a swathe of bronze and cherry red rudbeckias underplanted with creeping zinnias. I sowed the whole border for just $20, as a trial bed for *NZ Gardener*.

At the back of the hot border, the Mexican sunflowers (*Tithonia speciosa* 'Goldfinger') are glowing like molten lava. These vibrant shrub-like annuals are supposed to attract monarchs but I haven't seen a single butterfly this summer, unless you count the white cabbage butterflies whose chubby caterpillars are currently making a meal of my Brussels sprouts.

'Petite Bouquet' sunflowers

Dahlia 'Sharon Anne'

Mexican sunflower

Zinnias

Arrangement of sunflowers and 'Autumn Palette' amaranthus

Shirley poppy

Dahlia 'Aylestone Amethyst'

Dahlia 'Ruthie G'

'Petite Bouquet'

MY LATE SUMMER
FLOWER GARDEN
IS A JOY

AUTUMN

It's the beginning of the end
– time to pickle, preserve,
boil, brew and bottle . . .

Globe artichokes, apples and runner beans

'Italia' and 'Albany Surprise' grapes

Heirloom peans

'Schuyler' grapes

Peans and capucijner peas

AUTUMN HAS ARRIVED IN A HURRY. After a slow summer, it's as if everything has suddenly decided to ripen at once, including all the seed heads on the weeds. Neither the chooks, nor the compost heap, nor our fruit bowl, can keep up.

———— ‹‹◉›› ————

MARCH 1: Jason has a weakness for Wattie's Baked Beans. In a bid to wean him off them, I made my own baked peans for breakfast. He wasn't terribly impressed, although that could have been because, having not yet harvested a single tomato, I served them swimming in spicy plum sauce instead. It wasn't my finest culinary combination.

Dalmatian peans are white-seeded legumes that look like standard green climbing beans but have round, pea-shaped seeds inside their crescent-shaped pods. As far as I'm aware, the seeds are only available from Mapua Country Trading and the Koanga Institute.

It's possible to eat peans as a snap bean early in the season, though you have to be quick. The seeds swell so quickly that the pods rapidly resemble a small snake that's swallowed a packet of tennis balls.

MARCH 2: Mum's here helping me bottle apple sauce and peeling pears from my former garden in Western Springs, while Lucas's babysitter Melissa is pitching in and podding a mountain of dried Dutch peas. I cut down my capucijner vines and hung them to dry in my plastic propagating house, and the bright purple pods have now faded to the colour of blue ink stains on old wooden school desks.

Melissa's filled one bowl and is onto her second; I suspect we'll be eating a lot of pea and ham soup come winter.

MARCH 3: When my sister Brenda was pregnant, she craved grapes. Not just any grapes – certainly not those cruddy Chilean cheapies in our supermarkets – but ambrosial bunches of deep purple 'Albany Surprise' from Te Kauwhata. (Once, and only once, we made the mistake of driving through the Waikato township without stopping. Brenda refused to speak to us for days. Talk about the grapes of wrath.)

'Albany Surprise' has long been our family's favourite, though possibly only because 'Buffalo' is hard to come by. Its fruit is smaller and sweeter and, when made into a pie, its dark juice oozes out the edges to stain the pastry crust purple.

I've taken to pressing 'Albany Surprise' grapes into loaves of homemade focaccia. Let the dough rise up around the grapes, then drizzle with olive oil, sprinkle with sugar and bake till golden. We eat it hot from the oven, in fat slices dusted with icing sugar.

In my city garden, I wove the lanky vines of early-ripening, reddish-purple 'Schuyler' in and out of my front picket fence, but we've only got green grapes on the farm. Of all the green varieties, 'Italia', which ripens from dull green to amber in March, is my pick for musky flavour and vigour. It took only one season to swallow the compost bin and strangle an avocado tree in my city garden; on the farm our gnarled old vine has pulled apart a post and rail fence and high-tailed it up a pink-flowered horse chestnut tree. It sure makes them easy to pick.

MARCH 4: I've been bidding for old preserving jars on TradeMe. Another dozen arrived in the post yesterday so I'm bottling all my heirloom 'Blackboy' peaches before I head to Christchurch tonight for the Ellerslie International Flower Show. I'll be gone all week and I'm not sure the peaches will hold till I get back. I love bottling fruit, though I'll admit that my enthusiasm for today's task was somewhat tempered when I opened the door to discover that Mr Puppy Doo-Hawg had peed on the cardboard box overnight. His balls are on borrowed time.

Eighteen months ago I planted a pair of purple-fleshed 'Blackboy' peaches beside our chook run. Organic gardeners rave about their resilience and I can see why. My trees jostle for airspace with two disease-prone nectarine trees, yet despite holding hands, they've remained immune to fungal problems. Last year they produced just one peach each (which was more than I can say for any peach tree I've previously planted) but this year they've outdone themselves. I picked four dozen fuzzy fruit today. Though smaller than a 'Golden Queen', they're firm and freestone and make the most wonderful purple peach jam.

I'm full of respect for my hybrid 'Healey's Peacherine' trees too. I bought them on a whim and, like many of my horticultural flights of fancy, they sat in the driveway for six months while I ummed and aahed about where to plant them. In the end Jason took pity on them and dug holes on the bank below the asparagus bed. A year later, they're laden with golden fruit that, while not as fuzz-free as the label suggested, are full of flavour. Shame they're clingstone though; they're a pain to bottle.

One stone-fruit tree I'll definitely be ordering more of next winter is the nectarine 'Mabel'. My tree's a little lopsided – when the cows escaped in October, they chewed off half the branches – but even so it valiantly produced seven fruit in its first season.

And I didn't expect to get a crop of funny looking 'Flatto' peaches, so they're a bonus. In spring, my two-year-old trees fell victim to a shocking case of leaf curl – it was so bad I could see their red blistered foliage from the far end of our orchard paddock. As I don't use any sprays, I figured they were a lost cause, but I've picked enough fruit to bottle. (Okay, so I only had enough for one jar, but that's beside the point.)

'Flatto' peaches

'Mabel' nectarines

'Healey's Peacherines'

'Blackboy' peaches

MARCH 5: What an eerie experience it is to be in Christchurch for something as frivolous as a flower show when, one block back from the motel where Mum, Lucas and I are staying, the central city is slowly and depressingly being dismembered behind the red zone cordon. I was nervous about coming but it feels good to be here to support all the local gardeners, designers and growers. It's the least we can do.

MARCH 6: Against the odds, the Ellerslie International Flower Show has its mojo back. Hagley Park is in spiffing shape, with thousands of colourful hanging baskets dotted around the show grounds and, though most of the exhibits reference the devastating quake, the focus is clearly on the future.

The gardens are fantastic, and Lucas can't keep his fingers off them. He's a marigold and mulch magnet; I'm forever prising petals and bark chips out of his paws. My favourite exhibit is a wee vege patch designed by a Wellington student, Rachael Matthews. It comes complete with a clever composting system – just lift up the boardwalk planks and shove your green waste out of sight underneath; now that's my type of tidying! – and has exquisite natural obelisks from garlic flowers and toetoe. Her flax tepees in particular put mine to shame.

I ran into Maggie Barry at the opening night party. She congratulated me on my new role as a mum and I congratulated her on her new role as an MP. Then she asked me when baby number two was due. When I get home I'm burning my clearly not very flattering frock in our brazier!

MARCH 11: Aunty Jackie is selling apples from her Swannanoa orchard at the Oxford Farmers' Market, 50km north of Christchurch. I drove out there early this morning (any excuse for a slap-up brunch at Jo Seagar's café across the road). As I parked my car, I couldn't help but notice that the elderberry hedgerow between the council car park and the local butcher was laden with clusters of ripe berries. I can make Barry Dunnett's elderberry wine!

I find it impossible to resist a foraging opportunity, so Aunty Jackie gave me a couple of plastic bags and the chap selling sausages lent me a packing crate to stand on. As shoppers came and went, I acrobatically harvested 5kg of dark berries – enough to fill two supermarket bags – and snapped off half a dozen cuttings too. No one said a thing, except for a woman with an inquisitive miniature schnauzer named Alfie. 'Aren't you that lady off the telly?' she said.

Like blackcurrants and blueberries, elderberries are rich in antioxidant anthocyanins, and a daily swig of elderberry cordial is better than a flu jab for warding off winter ailments. My only hope is that all that juice doesn't leak out of the overhead luggage compartment on the plane home. I have visions of purple rain . . .

Rachael Matthews' show garden

derberries

MARCH 12: When I got married I vowed I'd never turn into one of those harridans who spell out, at length, their husband's flaws and foibles. But when I got home from the Ellerslie International Flower Show last night, I could have murdered mine. It was just getting dark as we drove into the driveway, but it wasn't dark enough to disguise the piles of felled branches – or the bald patches – along our formerly leafy liquidambar avenue.

I love the tunnel effect of our tree-lined driveway, but Jason won't tolerate the branches tickling his trucks. We'll never agree. So ladies, if you're thinking of marrying a man of the land, negotiate your own vows. Only promise to love, honour and obey if he agrees to keep his petrol-powered hedge trimmers and chainsaw under lock and key whenever you're away.

I'm not sure what Jason was eating while I've been in Christchurch, but it certainly wasn't courgettes. I've just filled a barrow with swollen marrows. Lucas thinks these caveman's club-sized courgettes are hilarious, but their relentless fecundity makes me despair.

As a teenager, I had a summer job picking courgettes. The money was good but it was the worst job I've ever had; worse even than disturbing people's dinnertimes as a telemarketer when I was a tertiary student. Picking courgettes was itchy, scratchy, back-breaking, boring work. And, what's more, having picked the field clean one day, you knew that three days later you'd be back to do it all over again.

I can't keep up with my courgettes this year – again. 'One plant per member of the family' is the advice I give to other gardeners, but it's a definite case of 'do as I say, not as I do'. I put in an entire packet of seed per member of our family this year, simply because I had extra space after my tomatoes succumbed to blight.

'Goldrush' courgettes

'Green Button' scallopini and cucumbers

'Greyzini' and 'Goldrush'

As well as standard green and gold courgettes, I thought it would be fun to mix it up with speckled 'Greyzini', lime-dipped 'Zephyr', heirloom 'Romanesco', cannonball-shaped 'Piccolo' and 'Green Button' scallopini.

Also known as pattypan squash, scallopini must be picked small – small enough to wrap your fingers around and enclose in your palm. Any larger and their flavour isn't so much subtle as insipid. I slice mine in half, rub them with a cut clove of new season garlic and grill them on the barbecue with a drizzle of lemon-infused olive oil and too much salt. Even then I wonder why I bother. They're the only vegetable I can think of that actually tastes better burnt.

If you let pattypan squash swell to the size of a discus, they're good for nothing but stuffing, though I've found a new use for them this summer. I've been flinging mine down the lawn like frisbees in a bid to teach the dog how to fetch. I wouldn't want to try that with my giant speckled 'Greyzini' marrows though. They'd knock his teeth out.

'Greyzini' is a cracker of a courgette, but turn your back on it for a day or two and it transmogrifies from a pert, finger-sized zucchini into a fat-bottomed blimp. 'It's as if someone has shoved a bike pump up its jacksie,' I emailed my colleague Robert Guyton. 'I'd hate to be standing beside one when it reached critical mass,' he joked in return.

Robert and I can be quite competitive. Our emails tend to escalate into one-upmanship: who picked the most peaches (me), who pressed the most apple juice (him), who grew the best garlic (the jury's still out). We've jokingly decided that our North versus South battle could make a jolly good book. We've got a working title – *Mine's Bigger than Yours* – and the battle lines have already been drawn. 'You'd have to let me win with anything that looks phallic,' says Robert, 'but you can have the rest.'

Kaye's zucchini jam

This is the most requested recipe from *NZ Gardener* magazine's archives. A few years ago, our call for clever courgette recipes was answered by Kaye Blaker, a Nelson gardener who has since shifted to Tauranga. Kaye's jam is delicious on toast, but even better as a sneaky substitute for lemon curd if you're making a lemon meringue pie.

Method: Chop 1kg golden courgettes (if using green courgettes, peel first) into rounds and steam until tender (I pop them in the microwave for a minute). Purée in a food processor until the pulp resembles custard. Place in a pot with 1kg sugar, the juice and finely grated zest of 3 lemons, and 125g butter. Stir until the sugar has dissolved, then simmer for 30 minutes, until the jam is thick and creamy, like lemon honey. Pour into hot, sterilised glass jars and seal. Unlike traditional lemon curd, which is made from eggs and needs to be consumed within a fortnight, this jam will keep in your pantry for 12 months.

Marrow mojito

It is possible to turn a courgette into a cocktail. All you need is a ripe marrow, a bag of brown sugar, a teaspoon of wine yeast, a packet of raisins and a pair of pantyhose.

Let the marrow ripen on the plant until its skin hardens and loses its shine and it sounds ever-so-slightly hollow when tapped. Then pick it, slice off the top, scoop out the seeds and any soft flesh, and stuff the centre with brown sugar, yeast and raisins. Put the top back on and seal the join with duct tape. Slip your stuffed marrow, stalk end up, into the pantyhose and tie to your garage rafters or hang inside your garden shed. Give it a prod every few days; when it's ready to drain the skin will start to feel a little squishy and it will start to leak. Use a pencil to poke a few holes in the bottom of the marrow and drain the juices into a bowl.

To make a marrow mojito, muddle fresh mint, a wedge of lime and a couple of sugar cubes in a tall glass. Add ice, a nip of your rotten marrow rum and top with soda.

Kaye's zucchini jam

Betty's potpourri

MARCH 13: I had to laugh at Kerre Woodham's Facebook page today. 'I found these white crawly things coming out of my brand new cupboards and I was about to nuke the house but it appears they're only pantry moths,' she wrote.

Only pantry moths? These antisocial butterflies were the bane of my life when I lived in the city. A female pantry moth can lay up to 300 eggs, which hatch into carbo-loading waxworms that eat anything starchy in sight, then spin cosy cocoons that look like scattered rice grains (very cunning). The blighters infiltrated my risotto rice, rolled oats and cereal, chewed through boxes of crackers and spiced up their sex lives by burrowing through my cinnamon quills, ground cloves and Spanish smoked paprika.

According to the *New Zealand Herald* today, Auckland is under attack. I'd believe it . . . because I've seen it. When I popped into the *NZ Gardener* office this afternoon, I shuddered to see beige and brown pantry moths flirting shamelessly in the storage area. They're hatching out of bags of birdseed we bought to make a DIY bird feeder a few months ago. (Mix together slightly warmed lard and smooth peanut butter, squish over an old pine cone, and roll in birdseed. Tie a string to the cone and hang from a tree.) As soon as I got home, I snipped a bunch of fresh bay leaves (*Laurus nobilis*) to hang in our pantry. Short of shifting house or calling in the exterminators, they're the only natural way I've found to keep *Plodia interpunctella* at, well, bay.

MARCH 14: When I first became interested in gardening, the crafty cottage craze was in full swing. I embroidered pillows with pictures of herbs, made my own natural hand creams and grew swags of English lavender and statice to hang from the rafters to dry. Then along came the low-maintenance trend and I pulled out my flowers, planted palms, succulents and bromeliads, and spent a small fortune on trailerloads of Kaiaua pebble.

Cottage flowers, thankfully, have since

Fresh bay leaves

made a comeback (though we call them bee-friendly wildflowers these days) but dried flowers and potpourri are now considered a bit naff. (Apparently the word naff is also a bit naff, according to the ladies at the local Country Women's Institute).

I still grow statice and everlasting daisies or helichrysums, but only for fresh cut flowers, and I doubt I'll ever make potpourri again. Why would I? It wouldn't be a patch on the exquisite package sent to me today by talented Southland gardener Betty Snell.

While talking to Betty about tussie-mussies, those adorable Victorian posies, the conversation turned to potpourri. 'Fusty, old-fashioned stuff,' I said. 'I'll send you some of mine,' she said.

It's a work of art, with pressed pansies, rose petals, lemon verbena leaves, scented geraniums, bergamot, marjoram and lavender. Inspired by dear old Olive Dunn, the Kiwi doyenne of cottage gardening, Betty dries petals in a fruit dehydrator till they're cornflake-crisp, then gently mixes them with orris root, non-iodised salt and essential oils of rose, honeysuckle and carnation, or cedarwood and lime with star anise and cinnamon. The end result looks – and smells – like an entire summer garden in a bowl.

MARCH 16: Jason had never eaten a fresh globe artichoke (*Cynara scolymus*) until I met him and, having checked these Mediterranean delicacies off his culinary bucket list, he says he'd rather not eat one again. He sighed when I returned home from the Clevedon Farmers' Market in spring with 24 silvery seedlings, and sighed again when I adopted another 20 sad seedlings – at $1 a pop, who could resist? – from the bargain bin at the local garden centre today.

Back when I was footloose and fancy free, I travelled to Europe most winters to attend the Chelsea Flower Show in London and the International Festival of Gardens in France's Loire Valley. In Paris, I'd buy fresh globe artichokes from the markets to steam in my motel room microwave and serve with garlic butter or vinaigrette.

Artichokes are easy to grow, and gorgeous at every stage. Their jagged silver foliage adds glamour at the back of my vege patch; the buds are architectural as well as appetising and, when I've had my fill, their nectar-rich thistle-like flowers are like heroin to honeybees and bumblebees. I love the flowers at the end of the season too, when their skeletons fade to the silvery hue of weathered macrocarpa.

I've grown globe artichokes in every garden I've ever owned but I've never seen a single self-sown seedling. Yet Mandy Villacorte, from Mandeville Gardens in Onewhero, reckons they're remarkably easy to raise from seed. I must give it a go next spring.

Globe artichokes with garlic butter

Harvest artichokes while the buds are still small – no bigger than your first – and tightly closed, leaving 2–3cm of stalk. Though artichokes are edible right up until the first peek of purple shows through, by then they'll have developed an inedible hairy choke in the centre that needs scraping out with a spoon. Squeeze the juice of a lemon into a bowl of water and, as you work, drop the trimmed artichokes into it to stop them oxidising and turning brown.

Use a sharp knife to trim off the top third of the bud, then peel the stalk and pull off the tough lower leaves. Steam whole, either in the microwave for 3–4 minutes or for 20–30 minutes over a pot of boiling water. When they're done, you'll be able to smell their aroma, and the leaves will peel off with no resistance. When cool enough to handle, serve with a bowl of garlic butter. Melt a thick slab of butter in a saucepan, add 2–3 cloves of crushed garlic and gently sauté.

Globe artichokes are messy to eat but that's at least half the fun. Use your front teeth to scrape off the fleshy base of each leaf as you work your way to the heart.

Artichoke flower

Globe artichokes

MARCH 17: Our neighbour Greg dropped around this afternoon with some tomatoes and a jar of homegrown honey from his hives. I tried to fob him off with some beans and marrows in return, but he wasn't having a bar of it – so I sent him home with a big bunch of flowers for his wife Michelle instead.

MARCH 20: I drove to Howick today to pick up a box of dusty Agee jars from a lady who was downsizing and clearing out her garage. I had to chuckle when I got home and took them out of the newspaper-lined box. The newspaper was a 14 February 1979 edition of the *Auckland Star*. She wasn't kidding when she said it had been a while since she'd last bottled fruit!

MARCH 23: Onion has gone broody again, and this time our little white hen has joined her. Onion has laid eight itty-bitty eggs in a hollow between the 'Damson' plum trees, while the little white hen is holed up in comfort in one of the nesting boxes in the henhouse. I suspect they're both wasting their time.

Sage, our rooster, isn't exactly Mr Machismo. A pedigree Chinese Silkie, he's the silliest looking rooster you ever did see, with a feathery fedora and fluffy feet. As a chick, he was mistaken for a girl (when I bought Sage and Onion, they were both supposed to be hens) but six months after I acquired them, Sage grew a wobbly comb and wattle.

I've seen Sage seduce Onion on several occasions – he hops on, squawks like a strangled cat, then hops off as if nothing had happened, leaving Onion looking slightly startled. However, given his short stature, I find it hard to believe he could have successfully impregnated the little white hen, so I lifted her off her nest today and – as advised by Google – tipped her upside down into a sack and gave it a good shake to snap her out of the motherly mood.

Sage

HE'S THE SILLIEST
LOOKING ROOSTER YOU
EVER DID SEE, WITH A
FEATHERY FEDORA AND
FLUFFY FEET

MARCH 25: It's Jason's birthday. He had hoped to sleep in but our stock agent had other ideas. So, while Lucas helped me make pancakes, Jason helped load a dozen of our fattest heifers onto the truck to send to the works. We're getting rid of them before winter, before we run out of grass and they start to lose condition.

One of the heifers has had a lucky reprieve. She's come down with woody tongue, a bacterial infection that causes excessive dribbling, so the local vet's coming around to prescribe antibiotics. Dad jokingly reckons that Lucas has woody tongue too. He could challenge that cow to a slobber-off. He must have some new teeth on the way.

MARCH 27: There are two questions that crop up time and again whenever I answer gardeners' calls on Newstalk ZB: 'How do I stop the neighbours' cats using my vege garden as a dirt box?' and, 'Why isn't my rhubarb red?'

As the owner of four cats (the most I've ever owned was six; had I not met Jason, I'd have carried on collecting them till I'd attained crazy cat lady status), I'm not too bothered where they do their business, provided it's not indoors.

When I lived in the city, I took it as a compliment when local cats came over to squat in my plot. My lovingly composted, carefully cultivated soil must have been Purex to their paws. But most gardeners aren't so magnanimous. On the radio, I advise callers to spray with the fungicide Thiram (its fragrance isn't appealing to felines); tie mothballs or tea bags soaked in kerosene to short stakes; cover seed trenches with chicken wire; or just concede defeat and get a small yappy dog. Clear nylon fishing line makes an excellent invisible barrier around newly cultivated beds, but having come a cropper tripping over it myself, I prefer to poke gooseberry bush and rugosa rose prunings around vulnerable beds. It works a treat – and they usually take root too, resulting in a puss-free patch and plenty of free plants to boot.

As for that ruddy rhubarb? The classic 'Victoria' strain has been weakened over the years as nurseries raise it quickly from seed rather than slowly by division. Most store-bought rhubarb plants either stay stubbornly green or ripen to streaky red around their necks if you're lucky. The only way to lay your hands on truly red rhubarb is to find another gardener with a jolly good clump and beg a chunk off the side – though that could be about to change. I've been sent a plant by Invercargill grower Peter Brass, of Evandale Gardens. It's a vigorous, productive new variety with slender shanks of ruby red right up to its neck. It doesn't have a commercial name yet, though *NZ Gardener* readers are plumping for either 'Scarlet Woman' or 'Redneck'. One deep south wit suggested 'Tim Shadbolt' as a suitable name.

Victoria' rhubarb

Ruby rhubarb champagne

This pretty pink fizzy drink requires red-stemmed rhubarb, though no one will be any the wiser if you sneak in a drop or two of red food colouring if need be.

Method: Chop 1kg red rhubarb stalks into inch-thick chunks. Place in a clean, 10-litre plastic bucket with 1kg sugar, 2 sliced lemons, ¾ cup cider vinegar and 6 litres filtered water. Cover the bucket with muslin cloth or a clean tea towel and stand for 2–3 days, stirring from time to time. Strain through a sieve (add the rhubarb to a pie) and bottle in clean plastic soft drink bottles. The champagne's ready to drink when the bottoms of the bottles start to push out with pressure. (You've left it too long if the bottles fall over or explode!) Chill well before opening carefully – twist the tops slowly to let the gas seep out or it'll fizz all over the place.

MARCH 28: I picked 20kg of tomatoes today. Okay, so I'm stretching the truth – I picked them up from Anthony and Angela Tringham's Clevedon glasshouse. Anthony and Angela, aka the Curious Croppers, run the tomato stall at the Clevedon Farmers' Market. They have a boutique business selling sweet, tasty tomatoes – just like the ones of old – to restaurants and cafés like Al Brown's award-winning Depot (if you see 'Little Horrors' on the menu, they've been grown by Anthony and Angela).

When I lived in the city, I had no trouble growing tomatoes. One year my 'Black Krim' tomatoes grew as tall as the lemon trees and produced more fruit than I could eat. By the end of the season, I had to sidestep hundreds of rotten tomatoes to get to my front door. But that was then, and this is now. My tomatoes have been a dead loss this year. Despite planting a mix of heirlooms and modern hybrids, in three successive plantings, they've all succumbed to blight. I haven't picked a single ripe fruit, or an unripe one.

Not to worry – I've cut a deal with Anthony and Angela: I get all the tomatoes I can eat, in return for a live sheep. I can't give them a dead one. It's against the law to trade with meat, and Section 67 of the Animal Products Act states that only the owner of an animal has the legal right to knock its block off to fill their freezer. However, there's a loophole that's also being exploited by so-called 'cowpoolers' (city slickers who band together to buy a whole cow to consume). Provided Anthony and Angela look after that little lamb for at least 28 days before it gets the chop, they can do the deed themselves.

I might not have grown them myself, but at least I won't have to buy any imported tinned tomatoes this year. I've bottled the lot today. Mum came over and together we turned my kitchen into a tomato processing factory, roasting, blanching, pulping, pickling, saucing (I use Annabel Langbein's Harvest Tomato Sauce recipe – it's the best pasta sauce recipe on the internet) and souping, if there's such a thing.

Because tomatoes are so low in acid, botulism bacteria can fester inside the jars if they're not properly preserved. I add citric acid to each litre jar of blanched tomatoes or whole cherry tomatoes and process them in my Agee automatic preserver, just to be on the safe side.

Preserved tomatoes

Whole tomatoes Score a cross into the blossom end of each tomato and dip in boiling water for 20–30 seconds; the skins then peel off easily. Pack into 1-litre sterilised preserving jars with 1 teaspoon sugar, 1 teaspoon salt and ½ teaspoon citric acid per jar. No extra liquid is required. Process in a water bath for 40 minutes. The method is the same for whole cherry tomatoes, though obviously you'd be mad to peel them all!

Roasted tomatoes Cut tomatoes in half and place in a roasting dish, cut side up. Sprinkle with salt, brown sugar and pepper. Roast at 180°C until the tomatoes are tender. Pack into warm preserving jars, add ½ teaspoon citric acid and process in a water bath for 15 minutes.

Tomato pulp Roughly chop tomatoes and bring to the boil. Simmer for 15 minutes, then take off heat and purée with a stick blender. Season to taste with salt and sugar. Bring back to the boil then pour into warm, sterilised jars. Add ½ teaspoon citric acid to each jar, seal and process in a water bath for 10 minutes.

'Black Cherry', 'Ace', 'Gold Nugget', 'Aunt Ruby's
German Green' and 'Tigerella' tomatoes

'Sweet 100' tomatoes

These perfect red tomatoes aren't mine – they're from the Clevedon Farmers' Market

TOGETHER WE TURNED MY KITCHEN INTO A TOMATO PROCESSING FACTORY

Old-fashioned tomato soup

This aromatic old-fashioned soup from the original Women's Division cookbook calls for exactly 7 cloves and 14 sprigs of parsley, but any quantity of sage, thyme and mint. The original recipe is thickened with 8 tablespoons of flour and half a pound of melted butter, but it's perfectly thick enough without it – and considerably lighter in calories! I also use it as a pasta sauce.

I've always thought this was the tomato soup recipe my mum used when I was a child. I remember her lining the top shelf of our pantry with dozens of bottles of soup for winter, but memories aren't always reliable. Mum reckons she has never made a jar of tomato soup in her life – she simply puréed a jar of bottled tomatoes and added a dash of cream to make her soup.

Method: In a very large soup pot, combine 6kg roughly chopped tomatoes, 6–8 roughly chopped onions, 1 cup sugar, 3 tablespoons cooking salt, 2 tablespoons celery salt (if you can't find it at your local supermarket, grind equal quantities of celery seed and salt), 2 teaspoons freshly ground black pepper, 7 whole cloves, 14 sprigs parsley, half a dozen sprigs of fresh thyme and mint and a few sage leaves (don't overdo the sage as it's quite pungent). Boil for an hour, then strain (I must get a mouli – I use a large mesh cake cover, upside down, to strain mine). Bring back to the boil and, working one jar at a time, ladle into warm, sterilised glass jars and seal immediately.

Clevedon Farmers' Market bruschetta

Hanging out at the farmers' market all morning would try the patience of any toddler but as soon as Lucas cut his first teeth, I found the perfect distraction: a crusty, chewy, bambina ciabatta bun from the bakery stall. It's always my first stop on a Sunday, not just to keep Lucas quiet but because ciabatta's the first ingredient on my list for this simple, summery, market-sourced bruschetta.

Start by buying a loaf of ciabatta from the bakery stall next to the coffee counter, then take four steps to the right to grab a pottle of fresh buffalo mozzarella or bocconcini from Helen and Richard Dorresteyn's Clevedon Valley Buffalo stall. Ask for a wedge of aged cheddar from Mount Eliza Cheese and choose a punnet (or two) of plum-shaped cocktail tomatoes from Angela and Anthony, plus fat cloves of organic garlic from Stella at Running Brook Seeds (she sells it as seed garlic but don't let that stop you eating it), a bunch of fresh basil from Phil and Jenny Tregidga of Clevedon Herbs and Produce and a bottle of River Estate Olive Oil, from Barry Wade's family farm at Whitford.

Method: Cut tomatoes in half, deseed, then dice and toss with finely chopped basil, a splash of balsamic vinegar, a drizzle of olive oil, sea salt and freshly ground pepper. Set aside for at least 10 minutes for the flavours to mingle.

Preheat your oven grill. Cut ciabatta into 1cm thick slices and arrange in a single layer on a baking tray. Crush or finely chop 1–2 large garlic cloves (I use my natty Turbochef pull-string mini food processor – if you ever get roped into attending a Tupperware party, take my advice and buy one!). Mix garlic with ¼ cup olive oil and brush over both sides of the ciabatta slices. Grill for a few minutes on each side, until golden brown.

Spoon the tomato mixture over the ciabatta; tear apart the fresh mozzarella and dot it evenly over the bruschetta, along with a sprinkle of finely grated cheddar. Return to the grill until the cheese starts to bubble.

Celia's pickled cherry tomatoes

This charming recipe for bottled cherry tomatoes with mint and garlic comes from *Cuisine* magazine food writer Celia Harvey, who tosses hers through pasta or serves them on antipasti platters. Celia uses red and yellow cherry tomatoes to give her pickles a bit more panache, plus brown sugar and cider vinegar, but I make a crystal clear pickling solution so my tomatoes look snazzier on the shelf.

Method: Lightly prick 1kg small, firm cherry tomatoes with a skewer. Pack tightly into 2 sterilised 1-litre glass jars, layering with fresh, unblemished mint leaves and 4–5 peeled garlic cloves per jar. In a saucepan, combine 200g sugar, 1 litre vinegar, 1 teaspoon salt and ½ teaspoon whole black peppercorns. Bring to the boil, stirring until the sugar has dissolved, then remove from the heat and cool completely. (I failed to read the instructions properly the first time I made these and bottled them in boiling vinegar, with no adverse effects – in fact I'd recommend this if you want to give your pickles away, as it seals the jars.) Pour vinegar solution over the tomatoes and gently push them down to prevent air pockets forming. Tap the jars with a spoon to raise any air bubbles. Seal and store in a dark, cool cupboard for 4–6 weeks before eating.

Clevedon Farmers' Market bruschetta

MARCH 30: I can't remember a summer when Mum didn't grow 'Scarlet Runner' beans on the frame along the path that led to our woodshed. She always grew too many and, though a young 'Scarlet Runner' is a joy to behold, with no strings attached, the geriatric beans are somewhat harder to swallow. My memories of Mum's 'Scarlet Runners' aren't exactly fond: by the end of the season, their curly pods were tough, fibrous and filled with floury seeds. She bottled, froze and salted them too, extending our misery into midwinter.

Is it any wonder that, when it came time to grow my own beans, I initially ignored trusty old 'Scarlet Runner' in favour of French green beans like dwarf 'Fin de Bagnols', or the beautiful butter bean 'Roquefort'? Even though 'Scarlet Runner' is one of the only true perennial vegetables, popping up year after year and getting few thanks for it, I wasn't tempted to grow my own until I saw a retro Spong bean slicer (one of those old ones that clamps to the kitchen bench and cuts the beans into perfect diamonds) for sale on TradeMe. It made me suddenly nostalgic for Mum's beans.

As well as sowing 'Scarlet Runners' this year I sowed its virginal sibling 'White Emergo'. It's such a beautiful bean, with blooms of pearly white instead of orange, as well as prolific: I've grown so many that today I bottled a basketful, just like Mum used to, and her mum before her.

BOTTLED BEANS ARE A FAR SIGHT NICER THAN SALTED BEANS

(I know I could just blanch them and bung them in the freezer, but where's the fun in that?)

Bottled beans don't taste like fresh beans, but they're a far sight nicer than salted beans (stack sliced beans in jars with a 1:2 mix of sugar and salt), which have to be rinsed and strained three times to retrieve any flavour. And when I popped the lid on my first jar of bottled beans, it took me right back to my childhood. Mum's beans weren't so bad after all.

MARCH 31: We all went to my sister's house in Onewhero today to celebrate Grace's fifth birthday. My brother-in-law Alan had put down a hangi in the paddock with a couple of chooks, cabbages, carrots, kumara, potatoes and a side of pork. We were supposed to have lamb too but my nephew Sam, when asked to give the dog a bone, found the $35 leg of lamb in the fridge and fed it to their English springer spaniel, Rocky. There were no complaints from the dog kennel.

Bottled beans

Top and tail 'Scarlet Runner' beans. Leave whole or slice, on the diagonal, into 3–4cm lengths. In a large pot, bring 2 litres water to the boil with 4 tablespoons white vinegar, 2 tablespoons plain salt and 2 tablespoons sugar. Simmer for 20 minutes (I have no idea what benefit is to be gained by such a long boiling time, but who am I to question Grandma Clarice's instructions?). Turn up the heat, add beans and boil for 3 minutes. Spoon into jars (work quickly), top up with the boiling solution and seal while hot.

Bottled 'Scarlet Runner' and 'Fin de Bagnols' beans

Feijoa wine

Bottled 'Pounamu' feijoas

Liquidambar leaf

APRIL 1: Working from home generally suits me to a T – I relish my sartorial slobbery and rarely bother to even brush my hair – but in feijoa season there are definite drawbacks, namely the lack of a communal lunch table from which to filch bags of fruit donated by desperate colleagues. (Autumn's first feijoas are a blessed thing, though by the end of May you can't even give the little buggers away.)

The motorway fruit shop at Bombay is selling new season's feijoas – big, fat, grenade-shaped fruit – for $10 a kg. I bought 15 bucks' worth today. 'Golly,' said the shop assistant. 'You have expensive tastes.'

I have no choice, for our tree is depressingly chaste. It has produced only eight fruit this autumn, though that's eight more than last year or the year before. I've read it its last rites: if it doesn't buck up its ideas next autumn, it's getting the chop. I'll replace it with 'Kaiteri' or 'Kakariki'. These Kiwi-bred varieties are among the first to fruit.

It's rare to encounter a feijoa with fertility issues but I've become acquainted with not one but two. In our garden at Onewhero, there were three trees of note on the side lawn: a scraggly native kowhai (I've never much admired them), a robust copper beech and a rotund feijoa that blossomed profusely every summer but produced diddly-squat in terms of fruit.

Feijoas fruit best in the company of others but our old tree couldn't claim to be lonely. Barely 20 metres away, on the other side of the paddock, our neighbours' tree was always laden. I've often wondered if the Masseys knew how many hours Brenda and I spent surreptitiously scrumping for fallen feijoas along the boundary fence.

I'm all for friendly thieving. Stealing fruit is such a wonderful way to get to know your neighbours (I rarely caught sight of mine in the city, though I did once catch the chap next door nicking avocados off my tree). And who knows, you might even stumble across your soulmate. I met a couple once who fell in love over a feijoa hedge. He was painting his roof when he spotted her pinching his fruit.

My best advice for would-be foragers? Get a dog. Not only does dog ownership give you a believable excuse for trespassing – 'Sorry, but I'm sure I saw my beloved Rover/Rocky/Rusty run past your rutabagas' – it also gives you a legitimate reason to carry plenty of plastic bags.

Julie's foolproof feijoa loaf

I'm of the firm belief that loaves – be they date, ginger, banana or feijoa – are simply an excuse to eat butter. (Much to the horror of my colleagues, and my coronary arteries, I have been known to use the cheese slicer on a cold block of butter.)

This luscious loaf is a one-pot wonder from North Shore gardener Julie Jackson. Preheat oven to 180°C. Peel and chop enough feijoas to yield 1 cup of flesh. Place in a pot with 1 cup boiling water, 1 cup sugar and 50g butter. Bring to the boil and simmer for 5 minutes, then take off heat and set aside to cool for a few minutes. Fold in 1 beaten egg, 2 cups self-raising flour and 1 teaspoon baking soda. Bake in a greased loaf tin for 40–50 minutes, until a skewer comes out clean. Serve warm with a big slab of butter or spread with lemon icing when cold.

Bottled feijoas

Feijoas are easy to preserve using the overflow method – and they lose none of their flavour. Peel and halve fruit, dropping them into a bowl of water with lemon juice added to stop the flesh turning brown. Bring a pan of light sugar syrup (1 part sugar to 3 parts water) to the boil and simmer feijoas until tender. Use a slotted spoon to gently scoop the fruit into warm, sterilised jars. Top up with boiling syrup and seal.

'Unique' feijoas are among the first to fruit each year

Linda's feijoa wine

Autumn wouldn't be the same without a few litres of feijoa wine fermenting in our hot water cupboard. This recipe comes from Linda Isbister, a Kumeu lifestyle blocker, and it's a cracker. My cousin Chris, a scientist at Lion Breweries, tested a sample of my latest vintage and reported back that it was 15.6 per cent alcohol with, in his professional opinion, a bouquet of apple, banana lollies and ethyl acetate (that's, ahem, the solvent in nail polish). I think it smells divine, and it tastes pretty fine too.

Scoop out the flesh (discard skins) from 5kg feijoas and freeze overnight. Thaw, squash and steep in a bucket with 6 litres boiling water and 2 Campden tablets (from home-brew stores). Cover the bucket with a tea towel and stand for three days, stirring occasionally, then strain, first through a large kitchen sieve and then through muslin cloth, to remove the gritty, gooey flesh. Pour the liquid into a fermenting vessel fitted with an airlock and add an 8g sachet of wine yeast, 2 teaspoons yeast nutrients, 4kg sugar and 2 litres cold water. Leave till it stops bubbling, then bottle.

Feijoa crumble

Preheat oven to 180°C. Peel, chop and quarter enough feijoas to line the base of a pie dish. Sprinkle with brown sugar and pop into the oven. While the fruit is heating, make the crumble topping. Combine 1 cup rolled oats, ½ cup flour, ½ teaspoon ground ginger and ½ teaspoon cinnamon in a bowl. Cut 100g butter into cubes and rub into the dry ingredients until the mixture's crumbly. Add ½ cup brown sugar, mix well, and sprinkle over the hot fruit. Bake for 30 minutes, or until the topping is golden.

APRIL 2: After a fairly ho-hum season, my strawberries are making a sudden late run for glory. I picked half a kilogram of large red berries this morning and there are still more to come. It appears that the netting tunnels I put over the plants in spring not only stopped the birds, but stopped the berries ripening until now too.

I boiled them up to make three jars of strawberry jam this morning, though it hasn't set so I've labelled it strawberry sauce instead.

'Camarosa' strawberries

APRIL 3: Autumn's here: the leaves have started to fall. As I walked up the driveway to get the mail today, liquidambar leaves in shades of gold, cherry, chestnut and copper floated down onto Lucas's stroller like slow-motion confetti. I could wander up and down our driveway all day and never tire of the sight.

Auckland's no Arrowtown, with its avenues of gilded foliage. When I lived in the city, about the nicest thing I could say about autumn was that it inoffensively bridged the gap between summer and winter. It wasn't hot, it wasn't cold – and it sure as anything wasn't colourful. Yet here on the city's rural fringe, though not exactly fiery, there are definite seasonal sparks. Our liquidambars, pin oaks, *Ginkgo biloba* and London plane trees are shedding their clothes as provocatively as Dita von Teese and, in the swamp, 10 of my *Nyssa sylvatica* trees are now glowing like beacons. The other two trees, subversively ringbarked by our sheep, are dead.

APRIL 4: The Tree Crops Association – a lively, likeable bunch of lifestyle blockers, orchardists and dendrologists – has elected me as their patron for the next 12 months. I announced my appointment on Facebook. 'Go plant a tree,' I said, 'and make it a productive one.'

I MADE THREE JARS OF
QUINCE JELLY AND TWO JARS
OF QUINCE JAM BEFORE
BREAKFAST THIS MORNING.

APRIL 5: I made three jars of quince jelly and two jars of quince jam before breakfast this morning. My friend Rachel's parents, Thelma and Peter Oldham, sent me a 9kg box of quinces, each fruit lovingly wrapped in tissue paper so it wouldn't bruise, from their garden in the Far North. The smell emanating from the box was incredible – aromatic quinces rival fully ripe pineapples for tropical perfume.

I must admit I was a tad overwhelmed when I opened the box, so I bundled it into my car, along with a box of preserving jars, and drove to Mum and Dad's for the night. Then Mum and I stayed up till midnight, peeling, coring, boiling and bottling them.

Quince jelly is as pretty as carnival glass, but it's time-consuming to make. Not quite as time-consuming as quince paste, which I've declared I'll never make again. Quince paste has to be simmered slowly for hours but my stove doesn't understand the meaning of slow. It invariably burns before it's done. Last year I made a batch in the slow cooker, then finished it off in muffin tins in the oven at 100°C, and though – 12 hours later – it turned out just like the bought stuff, I can't be bothered going through that rigmarole again!

It takes a bucket of quinces to make six jars of quince jelly. We hacked the firm fruit to bits with a meat cleaver and boiled it up in Mum's biggest soup pot but – isn't it always the way? – when it came to straining the pulp I realised I'd forgotten my jelly bag. We improvised, lining an old net curtain with a clean Chux cloth and hanging it off the rustic butcher's block in the middle of my parents' kitchen so the juice could drip into a mixing bowl on the floor.

It's the second year that Rachel's parents have sent me a box of quinces, but next year I should have enough of my own. My five 'Smyrna' trees all have a couple of fruit each this season. I'll use them to make quince chutney and quince vodka.

Scones

Dad loves quince jelly and so do I. Mind you, I'm a fan of any conserve that can be spread over a warm scone and buried under an obscenely large dollop of whipped cream. I make scones the easy way, mixing 4 cups self-raising flour with a 300ml bottle of cream, a can of lemonade, 1 tablespoon sugar and ½ teaspoon salt. Tip onto a floured board, cut dough into 12 squares and bake in a preheated oven at 220°C for 15–20 minutes, until golden. Scoff the lot hot.

Bottled quinces

Quince vodka

Quince chutney

Kelda's spiced quince chutney

This sweet chutney comes from Kelda Hains of Wellington's Nikau Café. I met Kelda last autumn at the capital's annual Jam Off competition – she and Al Brown were judging, while I was the very pregnant MC. Kelda makes preserves with panache and this spiced chutney is scrummy spread over cream cheese on crusty bread. No cardamom pods in your pantry? Substitute with star anise instead.

Method: Peel and core 1kg quinces. Place the peelings, cores and any other trimmings into a small stainless steel pot with just enough cold water to cover. Bring to the boil and simmer while preparing the remaining ingredients. Dice the peeled quinces and place in another pot with 1 large diced onion, 2 tablespoons grated fresh ginger, 3 cardamom pods, 1 cinnamon stick, 1 teaspoon salt, 200g white sugar and 150ml cider vinegar. Add 500ml of quince stock from the other pot. Cover chutney with a lid and simmer for 25 minutes, or until the quince is tender. Remove lid and simmer until the quince turns amber and the chutney thickens. If the liquid reduces too quickly, add more stock. Stir in 2 generous tablespoons honey and pour into sterilised jars. Seal. Makes 4–5 small jars.

Quince vodka

Wipe the fluff off 2–3 large quinces and either grate (watch your knuckles!) or pulverise in your food processor. Place in a large glass jar or a food-grade plastic container and sprinkle with ½ cup caster sugar. Add a bottle of cheap vodka and shake well. Store in a cupboard (I keep mine under the kitchen sink) and shake every few days for the first fortnight. Strain the liquid off the pulp after 3–6 months, though no harm comes to it if you leave it a full year.

Haw jelly

feasting on its fleshy autumn berries carelessly spread the seeds and now it's a weed.

We have self-sown hawthorns all through our gullies but they're rather hard to get to, which is why I prefer to stash my secateurs in the glovebox and go for a drive.

Last autumn I filled my car boot with haw berries. I found a recipe for haw wine and thought I'd give it a try. However, having plucked 1.5kg of berries, my enthusiasm waned when (a) I worked out how long it would take to de-stem and de-stalk those berries; (b) I kept stabbing my fingers on the thorns; and (c) I reread the recipe, only to find a scathing review from the brewer who published it in the first place. His verdict was unequivocal: 'the recipe sucks!'

So I found another recipe online for haw marmalade, and made that instead. It was so delicious, and so pretty, that I'm making it again today, along with a batch of haw jelly. My house has never smelled so sweet.

APRIL 6: I grew up in a close-knit community where everybody knew your name – I couldn't go for a brisk walk without someone stopping to offer a lift home. So I'm embarrassed to admit that, almost two years after moving to Hunua, I still don't know all my neighbours' names. (My initial efforts to infiltrate the local community came somewhat unstuck when, after I forced Jason to join a social netball team, he snapped his Achilles tendon in his first outing as goal defence.)

There are advantages to anonymity. I'm not ashamed to steal sky-blue hydrangeas from the hedgerow along Ararimu Road and no one knows that the lady standing on a stepladder under the hawthorns (*Crataegus monogyna*) on Hunua Road is me.

The common hawthorn is a little too common for its own good. Like gorse, it was introduced by early settlers to use as a hedging plant – and when it minds its manners, its thorny stems do make for a fine hedge. Unfortunately, birds

> ### Shelley's giant red haw and kumquat marmalade
>
> Shelley Jiang is a Beijing-based food blogger who uses giant hawthorn (*Crataegus pinnatifida*) to make this pretty red jam.
>
> **Method:** Fill a pot with ripe red hawthorn berries – use a fork to strip off the stalks – and add just enough water to cover. Simmer, covered, for 45 minutes, till the fruit is soft enough to gently crush with a potato masher. Strain pulp through a jelly bag and let drip overnight. While the haw juice is draining, thinly slice 5 kumquats or 1 grapefruit and stand overnight in a small bowl of water.
>
> The next day, measure the haw juice and pour into a pot with an equal volume of sugar and the drained citrus. Boil till it reaches setting point.

Fresh chestnuts from Chestnut Charlie's, and my mate Paul's macadamias

APRIL 8: On the road to Clevedon there's a pick-your-own chestnut farm called Chestnut Charlie's where, if you bring your own bag, you can forage for fallen nuts for $3 a kg. As our chestnut trees are a few years off flowering, I stopped on the way home from the farmers' market today. I wore my gumboots: the least painful way to release those glossy brown nuts from their kina-like burrs is to stomp on them.

Chestnuts are magnificent trees. Hardy too. They can shrug off winter frosts to -25°C, though late spring frosts can damage their swelling buds, wet soils rot their roots and possums and rabbits nibble their shoots. I planted five trees to ensure the best possible pollination. The varieties '1002' and '1015' are compatible, though a rather unromantic sounding couple, and '1005' is self-fertile but still prefers the company of '1002'.

I'd rather grow macadamia nuts than chestnuts, though I suspect it's too frosty here – and anyway, my work colleague Paul has a macadamia orchard near Waiuku and he sells them at work for $5 a bag, so we're never short of nuts to roast.

Nat King Cole crooned about chestnuts roasting on an open fire, but a barbecue plate is better. I use a sharp knife to score a cross in the shell of each nut to let out the steam as they cook. Skip this step and they self-combust, which is funny inside an oven but downright dangerous if you're within firing range outdoors.

It takes 15–20 minutes for chestnuts to roast. The shells pop open when they're done. I add butter – lots of butter, season with salt and set aside for a few minutes to cool slightly. There's nothing worse than buttery burnt fingers, except a buttery burnt tongue.

NAT KING COLE CROONED ABOUT CHESTNUTS ROASTING ON AN OPEN FIRE, BUT A BARBECUE PLATE IS BETTER

'Golden Nugget' 'Delicata' squash 'Musquee de Provence'

APRIL 11: My pumpkin patch has performed poorly this year. From an entire packet of seed, I've picked just one miserable 'Triamble' – a grey-skinned heirloom with unusual triple-lobed fruit. I remember my Uncle John growing 'Triamble' pumpkins as big as footstools, but my solitary gourd could barely double as a doorstop.

Granted, I was late sowing the seed, but I suspect my 'Musquee de Provence' and 'Marina di Chioggia' aren't going to ripen fully unless we get a miracle in the form of a sunny May.

The striped cream squash 'Delicata' has been a delight, but its gourds are no bigger than cucumbers. At least the miniature 'Golden Nugget' hasn't let me down. It's a non-trailing variety, like a courgette, and each of my plants has produced half a dozen glowing orange pumpkins. When I took them to the market, at least half my customers confessed to buying them as table decorations!

As if the lacklustre summer wasn't bad enough, my plants have suffered terribly from powdery mildew this autumn. While moaning about it to Stella at the Clevedon Farmers' Market, she whispered two words to me: 'Liquid Gold'. It's the title of a book by Carol Steinfeld, an eco-entrepreneur who advocates the use of urine as a garden fungicide (diluted 1:10 with water) and fertiliser (diluted 1:20). Apparently neat urine can also be used as a clean-up spray to kill fungal spores on deciduous fruit trees in autumn, just before the leaves drop. I'm tempted to give it a go, though it really strikes me as a man's job . . . a man with exceptionally good hand–eye coordination.

I ASSUME THE TOADSTOOLS ARE TOXIC, BUT I'M TEMPTED TO TRY THE PUFFBALLS

APRIL 14: When I took the dogs for a run this afternoon, I came across a fairy ring of spotted toadstools under the pine trees. It must be a fertile season for fungi, because puffballs are popping up on the shady side of the driveway too. When I jump on them, they explode with a satisfying pop into a cloud of fusty-smelling pixie dust.

I assume the toadstools are toxic, but I'm tempted to try the puffballs. A few years ago,

I went foraging with restaurateur Fleur Sullivan at Moeraki. She took me to a local farm where she'd found giant puffballs (*Calvatia gigantea*) as big as basketballs – we could only fit three in our car boot – huddled in a ring like a spongy Stonehenge.

That night at Fleurs Place, her chef sliced the puffballs, rolled them in garlicky crumbs (with black speckles that may or may not have been bits of dried seaweed) and fried them in pizza-

sized wedges. Their flesh was as firm and white as a sponge-rubber mattress. We ate them with Cullen Skink (which you'll be relieved to know is not an endangered gecko but a creamy smoked fish soup from Scotland) and fresh moki.

But I digress. Were Jason to read this page over my shoulder, he'd accuse me of running fast and loose with the truth. Not about the puffballs – he knows I'll eat anything once if I think it'll make a story – but about the run. So, let the record state that only the dogs ran. I sat on a big log at the bottom of the hill (a log Jason carved with his initials after carting it into place as a horse jump a decade ago), and tickled Lucas under the chin with a buttercup bloom. As his skin glowed golden I asked, just as I remember my parents asking me, 'Do you like butter?'

Like whistling with a blade of grass wedged between your thumbs, the buttercup quiz is one of the simple pleasures of a country childhood – but I've ruined the memory now. I googled it. Turns out that scientists at the University of Cambridge have discovered a perfectly rational explanation for generations of glowing chins.

According to a study published in the Royal Society journal *Interface*, and referenced on the university's website, 'the buttercup petal's unique bright and glossy appearance is the result of the interplay between its different layers. In particular, the strong yellow reflection responsible for the chin illumination is mainly due to the epidermal layer of the petal that reflects yellow light with an intensity that is comparable to glass.'

I won't tell Lucas any of that, but I will spread a little extra butter on his toast tomorrow morning.

APRIL 16: It's time I stopped questioning my menfolk's virility: Lucas was a surprise conception, our cows all calved on cue, Rambo's sly seductions reaped an easy $1500 this year and – wonders will never cease! – Sage isn't shooting blanks after all.

In her fourth attempt, my Chinese Silkie Onion has become a mum. She's puffed up with pride, propped up in a bed of hay in a fruit crate in our hot water cupboard with seven chicks under her wing. I've named them Garlic, Leek, Chive, Shallot, Scallion, Spring Onion and 'Pukekohe Longkeeper'. One egg failed to hatch, which is probably just as well. I was running out of allium species.

It's almost a year to the day since that same fruit crate was pressed into service as a maternity ward for our mama duck, Streaky Beak. She hatched seven caramel custard-coloured ducklings under the barberry hedge on our boundary and led them through the swamp to show them off to us. Concerned that the hawks would pick them off, I bundled them into the red barn with a bowl of chicken crumbles and an old kitty litter tray with a couple of inches of water in the bottom. Like a duck to water, or so I thought.

Twenty-four hours later, six of the seven were dead. Three drowned (they could get into the water, but with no proper wings and only stumpy webbed feet, they couldn't get out again), Streaky Beak squashed two more in the resulting melee and the sixth was simply missing in action.

I cried like a baby, because it wasn't the first time my attempts to intervene in the nature versus nurture debate had unexpected consequences. When my sister and I were in our teens, we rescued two baby bunnies that had been buried alive when our cows had caved in the entrance to their burrow. We raised those rabbits in a big cardboard box that we'd conscientiously lock away in our bedroom while we did our chores. Except one afternoon the cat wised up and got there first, biding its time under the bedspread. By the time we discovered our error, both rabbits were dead.

I've vowed to do better with Onion's brood (though if they all prove to be roosters, I'll have to eat them). I've sent Jason off to pick up a rat-proof, dog-proof, hawk-proof, cat-proof coop from Maureen's mate Rob. I'll clear a space for it in my vege patch and Onion and her babies can start earning their keep by fertilising my soil for next season.

Onion and Chive

Streaky Beak's ill-fated babies

APRIL 22: Having been roped into a speaking engagement at a Rotary conference at Waitangi this weekend, Jason and I drove to Kerikeri for a whistle-stop tour of the Bay of Islands Farmers' Market this morning. I bought a bag of Dalmatian elephant garlic, a wedge of Mahoe Farmhouse cheese, half a dozen chunky orange capsicums . . . and a perfect wee pineapple. The pineapple was grown by Jan Tagart and Steve Cottis in a tunnelhouse north of Kaeo. Jan started with just two plants – her chiropractor gave her a couple of cuttings from a potted plant in her practice – and now has several hundred fruiting plants.

It takes a lot to make me jealous, horticulturally speaking, but paeonies, pomegranates and pineapples will do it. I've tried and failed to grow all three. Every year when I return from Hunter's Garden Marlborough in November I test the patience of Air New Zealand's cabin crew by trying to bring home an ever-bigger bunch of herbaceous paeonies. My favourite varieties are 'Sarah Bernhardt', a double shell pink with flecks of cerise, and blood-red 'Red Charm', both of which I've optimistically planted by our back door. Neither flowered last spring, though 'Red Charm' did send up a solitary bud the year before. The climate's simply not to their liking here, though in Granddad's day, cream paeonies bloomed along the front of the farmhouse at Onewhero. I can say this for sure because I recently found dozens of paeony photos in an old box of his slides.

I won't bother to plant a pomegranate tree here. I've never seen one fruit satisfactorily in New Zealand, though on holiday in Portugal a few years back I was amazed to see laden pomegranate hedgerows lining rural roadsides like our ubiquitous barberry. In my city garden, my scrappy shrub produced just one pitiful flower in five years. What's worse, I was so excited that, while pointing it out to a friend, I accidentally knocked off the bud with my finger.

I'd rather grow pineapples than pomegranates anyway – and now I can. I've saved the spiky topknot to replant in a pot of propagating sand in my hothouse. Pineapples are child's play to raise this way, but you can't pull it off with a supermarket fruit anymore. They're all given a short back and sides trim before they're allowed into the country.

APRIL 23: I can't keep up with all the passionfruit plopping off our vine. We're scooping the tangy pulp over vanilla ice cream most nights, yet still their wrinkled fruit pile up in the fruit bowl. (Speaking of wrinkles, my niece Grace recently asked Mum what the lines on her face were. 'Wrinkles,' Mum explained. 'Do they hurt?' worried Grace.)

We can't eat all the passionfruit I'm picking so I've been bottling the pulp. For every 2 cups of pulp, I add a generous cup of sugar (not too much though, or you end up with jam). Boil for a couple of minutes then pour into small jars, seal, and process in a water bath – I use a deep soup pot – for 5 minutes.

Bottled passionfruit

APRIL 24: Every Friday I write an e-newsletter for *NZ Gardener* called *Get Growing*. In last week's edition, I made a birth announcement on Onion's behalf – and then asked for help naming her chicks' new nursery. Martha Stewart's fancy-pants henhouse is called Le Palais des Poulets and I've heard of other chook houses with cute names like Cluckingham Palace, but I can't think of anything that suits my Silkies.

Our email inbox is now overflowing with witty ideas and ostentatious offerings in several languages, including Latin. (From now on, instead of yelling out 'here, chooky, chooky' when I fling them their mash, I shall holler 'come and get it, *Gallus gallus domesticus*'.)

My favourite suggestions include: A Box of Birds, Broody Boudoir, Bunch of Onions, Chez Chook, Chicken Chalet (spoken with a soft 'ch' so it sounds posh), Coop-a-cabana, Egg Plant, Fowlty Towers, Hatchington Hotel, Impeckable Palace, La Maison de l'Oignon, Merinque Motel, Peckingham Palace, Silkie House of Disrepute (Sage might have something to say about that), Silkie Suite, Taj Ma-hen or Taj Ma-chook, Te Whare Pikaokao, The Funky Chicken, The Hentagon (if only it wasn't a triangular A-frame hutch), The Onion Patch (or, en français, Le Jardin d'Oignon), The Hunua Hennery, Tres Chick, Whare Ma or Wuji Huang Gong (a Chinese imperial palace for Silkie chooks).

But I laughed loudest at Leigh gardener Terry Healey's idea: the Hunua Henitentiary.

APRIL 25: How appropriate, on ANZAC Day, to waken to a dawn service. Except it wasn't the sound of a solitary bugler ringing out across the valley as the sun rose, but an almighty scrap by squawking magpies. They're such aggressive, beastly birds. My childhood cat Biggles caught a baby magpie once. We heard her yowling for mercy as its parents dive-bombed her, pecking and scratching, until she let it go. She never made that mistake again.

Every year on ANZAC Day I sow a packet of red soldier poppy (*Papaver rhoeas*) seed, and today was no different. Lest we forget.

ONION'S BABIES ARE LOCKED UP FOR NOW, BUT AS SOON AS THEY'RE BIG ENOUGH TO OUTWIT THE DOGS AND CATS, I'LL LIBERATE THEM INTO THE ORCHARD

Fresh hop cones weigh next to nothing

APRIL 26: My arms are itchy from picking hops, but I'll sleep like a baby tonight. Hops (*Humulus lupulus*) have been prized as a herbal sedative since Pliny was a boy, though I'd rather drink them than sink my head onto a pillow stuffed with their aromatic, papery flowers. Hops have been used to brew beer since the fourteenth century but King Henry VIII later outlawed them, declaring them to be 'a wicked weed that would spoil the taste of the drink and endanger the people'.

The first time I tried to grow hops, along bamboo trellis at the edge of my city deck, snails chewed my 'Smooth Cone' vines down to the ground before they ever had a chance to flower. When I moved to Hunua, I transplanted the dormant crowns into the bed in front of the stables, gave them a shovelful of blood and bone, and left them to it. Six months later, they'd risen from the dead to reach the roof.

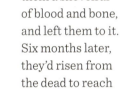

EVEN IF I WAS A TEETOTALLER I'D STILL GROW HOPS

I'm partial to a homegrown summer shandy, but even if I was a teetotaller I'd still grow hops. The vines burst from the soil in mid-spring with admirable alacrity – according to an organic hop farmer in Tapawera I interviewed a few years ago, a well-fed vine can put on 15cm growth in 24 hours – and the foliage is lush and decorative.

My vines start to flower in January and, last autumn, they were prime for picking in March; but they've been slower to ripen this year, probably due to the sad excuse we had for a summer. Ripe hop cones are slightly sticky, have a strong aroma and look like miniature green armadillos. I picked enough today to fill a 10-litre bucket – double last year's crop – but even so they weigh next to nothing; my harvest tipped the scales at 260g.

Heather's hop beer

At Mapua Country Trading, Heather Cole includes this hop beer recipe with every hop vine she sells. It requires 120g hop flowers, either fresh or vacuum-sealed and frozen.

Method: Simmer 90g hop flowers in a large pot of water, covered, for 45 minutes, then add another 30g of hops and boil for 15 minutes. Strain the liquid into a clean 20-litre container, add 1.5kg brown sugar, 500g honey, 2 tablespoons treacle, 1 teaspoon citric acid and the juice of 2 lemons (preferably 'Yen Ben' or 'Lisbon'). Shake or stir until the sugar and honey have dissolved, then fill up the container with warm filtered water (no hotter than 20°C). Stir in a sachet of beer maker's yeast and fit the container with an airlock to let the gas out, but stop vinegar flies getting in.

Clear space in your hot water cupboard as hop beer needs to be kept warm (20–25°C) for 7 days to keep the fermentation chugging along nicely. The beer's ready to bottle when it stops bubbling; add a teaspoon of sugar or a carbonation tablet to each bottle to foster some fizz. Store for a month before drinking.

Hop beer

Amaranthus 'Autumn Palette'

AMARANTH IS HAILED AS A NUTRIENT-RICH SUPERFOOD

APRIL 28: My garden's winding down, easing up, limping slowly and sadly towards the end of the season. If I had to describe my vege patch in one word, this week it would be shabby. My dwarf beans have seen better days, the last row of 'Cos' lettuces has gone to seed, my eggplants are ragged, the birds have gutted the sunflower heads, my dahlias are all dusted with powdery mildew and the courgettes at the far end of the garden have collapsed, exhausted, over the stone kerbing and onto the lawn. The only thing that's actively growing is my compost heap.

I'm going to the farmers' market tomorrow but all I have to sell are several buckets of Jerusalem artichokes, 'Chicago' sweetcorn, the last of my chillis, a bowl of early Brussels sprouts, a basket of 'Golden Nugget' pumpkins, cavolo nero, 'White Belgian' carrots as big as parsnips, and the colourful silverbeet known as Swiss chard.

Not that there's any point picking the chard. No one buys it. I'm not convinced that anyone even eats it. We certainly don't. I've got two burgeoning rows of 'Bright Lights' silverbeet, half of which has gone to seed. The cows are in the house paddock today so Jason gave me a hand this afternoon to pull out most of that seedy silverbeet and biff it over the fence. While he was busy doing that, I whipped inside to grab a paper bag to shake my amaranth seed into.

Amaranth, like quinoa and millet, is a heritage grain that's hailed as a nutrient-rich superfood. I put in two types – the copper coloured ornamental variety 'Autumn Palette' (which, incidentally, is edible too) and a red type given to me by Mandy Villacorte at the Clevedon Farmers' Market. Both grew at least 1 metre tall, with fluffy seed heads like foxtails.

Amaranth is apparently delicious toasted, sprouted, added to bread or boiled up to make a form of porridge, but I'll have to wait until next year to find out. Remind me never to leave my man unattended in the vegetable garden: by the time I got back with my paper bag, Jason had fed all my seedy amaranth to the cows too.

APRIL 30: If an apple a day keeps the doctor away, we won't need to see our GP again until 2014. I've got a superb, if somewhat lumpy and scabby, haul of organic green 'Granny Smith' apples – I've already bottled eight litres of apple sauce – and this afternoon Lucas and Jason helped me pick the last of the 'Libertys'. I'd leave them on the branches a little longer but the birds are starting to peck holes in their skins.

Apples are so easy to grow here. I've planted too many already, but I rather fancy a few more, starting with the old-time cider varieties like 'Slack ma Girdle', 'Brown Snout', 'Broxwood Foxwhelp' and 'Hoary Morning'. For now, I pick 'Jack Humm' and 'Jelly King' crabapples to give my cider a tart kick. 'Jack Humm' is a spitting image of those small fake red apples sold as Christmas decorations, while 'Jelly King' has blushing orange/red fruit that the birds leave well alone. Both varieties make a lovely amber jelly, as clear as a glob of kauri gum, not to mention teeny-tiny, sweet-and-sour toffee apples.

Toffee apples are never as nice as you think they're going to be. Not just because you end up with sticky gloop all over your face, but because the toffee's generally too sweet to eat in such a large dose, and the apple is invariably all soft and mushy underneath. Which is where the crabapple really comes into its own: crabapples stay crisp and tart under a glossy coat of toffee.

Apples are so adaptable, and they're no hassle to prepare. I've got a Chinese-made apple peeler that strips, slices and cores them with the crank of a handle, spitting out a stark-naked apple slinky every seven seconds. These nifty gadgets are all over TradeMe, though I bought mine from the Riverton Environment Centre. Best $27.50 I've ever spent.

The chooks clean up the cores and the ribbons of peel, while we enjoy apple sauce with roast pork, spicy apple butter stirred through porridge, speedy cider and Grandma Pat's famous apple shortcake. I rang her up to get her recipe. 'A fair bit of butter, flour, sugar, baking powder and an egg,' she said.

When butter was in short supply, Grandma attempted to make puff pastry with mutton fat. She invented her own apple turnover recipe, spicing the fruit with cinnamon and nutmeg in a bid to disguise the flavour of the fat. 'I never quite achieved it,' she confesses, half a century later, 'but the shearers didn't seem to mind.'

IT TOOK 12 HOURS FOR MY NIÈR BEURRE TO TURN INTO THICK BROWN SLUDGE

Nièr beurre (Jersey apple butter)

This spicy, treacle-coloured preserve dates back to the 1500s and is a by-product of the Channel Islands cider industry. The traditional method is to simmer it for 30 hours, stirring constantly, in huge copper cauldrons over an open fire. You know it's done when a wooden spoon, pressed into a sticky dollop on a plate, adheres sufficiently to lift the plate. I make a scaled-down version in my slow cooker.

The first time I made it, I posted about it on my blog. 'It took 12 hours for my nièr beurre to turn into thick brown sludge,' I wrote, adding 'Anyone care to translate that into Jersey's Norman–French dialect?'

The next day, L'Office du Jèrriais – the organisation dedicated to promoting the Jersey language – got in touch. 'Lé v'chîn en Jèrriais (Here it is in Jèrriais),' they wrote. 'V'là tchi prînt douze heuthes pouor qu'man nièr beurre s'nièrchîsse et s'affêtchîsse.' Try saying that after a few ciders!

Method: Cook 4kg peeled, sliced cooking apples in 500ml fresh apple juice or dry, homemade cider for a few hours, till the apples turn mushy. Add ½ cup caster sugar, a 40g log of natural liquorice, the zest and juice of 1 lemon, 1 teaspoon ground cinnamon and 1 teaspoon mixed spice. Give it a good stir before you retire for bed and, when you rise in the morning, you'll have apple butter to spread on your toast.

Nièr beurre

Positioning five 'Peasgood Nonsuch' apples at the top of the terraced bank below our house may not have been my smartest move. In their first season, each tree has spawned a trio of jumbo fruit, each weighing just shy of half a kilogram. But, one by one, they started disappearing. At first I thought possums must be pinching them, but the discovery of a bruised and battered apple on a race down by the cattle yards suggests that Newton's laws of motion are to blame. These rolling pommes are gathering not moss but momentum as they plunge down the hill, across the equestrian arena and down through the flax. Perhaps I should abandon my plans for a fancy French garden and build a tenpin bowling alley instead.

THESE ROLLING POMMES ARE GATHERING NOT MOSS BUT MOMENTUM AS THEY PLUNGE DOWN THE HILL

Ray McVinnie's Torta di Mele

I cut this recipe out of *Sunday* magazine a year ago and have lost count of the times I've made it since. It's the only reason I bother to save my own fennel seeds. Torta di Mele is a perfect autumn pudding, served with either whipped cream or homemade vanilla ice cream, and – like steamed puddings and spare apple dumplings – it's even better, if there's any left, for breakfast the next day.

Ray describes it as 'an old-fashioned, country-style, Italian way to make a cake. It's simply a batter holding together sliced apples. When you think it's cooked, leave it in the oven a bit longer to ensure it's well done or the juice from the apples will make it rather wet once it's cool.'

Method: Preheat oven to 180°C. Grease a 23-cm diameter loose bottomed cake tin and line with baking paper. Beat 100g butter and 100g caster sugar until pale and creamy. Beat in 3 eggs, one at a time. Stir in 1 teaspoon vanilla extract, the zest of 1 lemon, 2 teaspoons fennel seeds, 100g flour and 1 teaspoon baking powder, then fold in 4 thinly sliced apples. Spoon batter into the cake tin and let sit for 10 minutes, then sprinkle with extra caster sugar and bake for 45–50 minutes.

'Granny Smith' apples

Walter the Saint's speedy cider

Traditional cider takes months to ferment, but a couple of years ago I came across a recipe online for speedy cider – it's ready in two weeks and can crack 10 per cent alcohol. I got it from Kathy Haynes at the Harvington Imbibers Club (HIC!) in Worcestershire. 'The lofty aim of our little dedicated band of liver-abusers is the pursuit of cheap, tasty booze,' admits Kathy. She acquired the recipe from her son, who procured it from a paramedic dressed as a saint at a historical re-enactment club meeting.

Bung a 1.5kg bag of cooking apples into your freezer for 3 days. Thaw until soft enough to pulp – skins, cores and all – in batches in a blender (add water if you fear for your blender's motor). Pour pulp into a clean 10-litre bucket and top up with 5.7 litres of filtered water. Loosely fit a lid, or cover with a clean tea towel and stand for 7 days, stirring twice daily. Strain through muslin cloth and pour the juice back into the bucket, along with 1kg sugar and the zest and juice of 3 lemons. It should start fizzing in the bucket 48 hours later. Strain again and bottle in screw-top plastic bottles so you can loosen the lids if they threaten to blow.

Mum's caramel apple dumplings

Preheat oven to 180°C. Peel and core 4 cooking apples. Sift 2 cups flour, ½ teaspoon baking powder and ¼ teaspoon salt into a bowl. Rub in 110g butter and a little water to make a firm dough. Divide dough into 4 pieces and roll out. Wrap each apple in dough and place in a deep pie dish. In a small jug, combine 50g melted butter, 1 cup sugar and ½ cup boiling water. Stir well and pour over apples. Bake for 40 minutes, basting regularly, until the pastry is golden.

CIDER FROM A PARAMEDIC DRESSED AS A SAINT

'Liberty' apples eventually ripen fully to dark red

Grandma Pat's apple shortcake

Peel, core and slice 4–6 apples and stew with a little water, lemon juice and sugar. If your apples are small, use more: there's nothing worse than an apple slice with a stingy smear of fruit in the middle. When the apples are tender, take off the heat and strain.

Preheat oven to 180°C. Rub 125g butter into 2 cups sifted flour. Add 1 teaspoon baking powder, 1 beaten egg, 3 tablespoons sugar and just enough milk to form a firm dough. Divide dough in two. Roll out half to line a sponge roll tin. Spread evenly with apple then roll out the remaining dough and, defying the laws of gravity, place it on top. 'It's a cow of a thing to do without breaking it,' advises Grandma.

Prod shortcake with a fork and bake for 20 minutes. When cool, sprinkle with icing sugar and cut into even squares (to avoid squabbles).

'Jelly King' crabapples

Toffee crabapples

Wipe the apples clean, twist out the stalks and impale them on kebab sticks. To make the toffee, combine 1 cup sugar, 3 tablespoons water, 1 teaspoon cider or white vinegar, 1 teaspoon butter and a couple of drops of red food colouring in a small pot. Bring to the boil, stirring until the sugar has dissolved, then boil for 2–3 minutes, until a small dribble dropped into a cup of cold water turns hard and thread-like. Don't take your eye off it as it turns from red clear toffee to burnt brown caramel in a matter of seconds. Take the pot off the heat, tilt it to one side and dip the apples in individually, giving them a slow spin to evenly coat in toffee. Place on a tray lined with baking paper to set.

Me, Jason and Lucas picking the last of the 'Liberty' apples

Hydrangeas

MAY 1: Jason's hoping Lucas will grow up to be a strapping lad – his dream is for Stonedale Civil to one day become Stonedale Civil & Son – but I have my doubts. The little fellow can't move fast enough to get his fingers on my flowers. When he took his first steps outdoors, he didn't walk towards his father or mother. No, he wobbled unsteadily across the lawn to grab a fistful of dwarf zinnias.

How disappointed Lucas will be next month, when there are no flowers left to pick. The garden is winding down for winter. The oak trees are letting go of their leaves and every morning a little more of the Hunua Ranges is revealed through their filigreed foliage. The pin oaks and plane trees around the swamp are positively pyrotechnic – viewed from a distance at least – but up close, my dahlias are downcast and dishevelled, my roses riddled with black spot and all the russet red rudbeckias have died without dignity. Only my hydrangeas have the decency to age gracefully.

Jason thinks hydrangeas are hideous. He says they remind him of toilet brushes, which I find amusing – like most men, I'm not convinced he actually knows what a toilet brush looks like.

Unlike Jason, I adore them all, from the blobby blue moptops of old to the pomegranate-red 'Merveille Sanguine', a variety a Taranaki nurseryman renamed 'Bloody Marvellous'. For our wedding, I planted two dozen 'Bridal Bouquet' hydrangeas under the horse chestnut tree in front of our house. They start the season crisp white and virginal but end up sullied and splotchy pink. I think I prefer them that way.

I prune and pick the season's last hydrangeas, cutting their flower stems down to a pair of fat buds, and pile them into vases around the house. They're a doddle to dry for winter arrangements – just don't add any water to the vase.

ONLY MY HYDRANGEAS HAVE THE DECENCY TO AGE GRACEFULLY

Single-flowered dahlia

MAY 2: I've just spent a pleasant afternoon in the nuttery – as I have pompously taken to calling the 20 almond and five chestnut trees on the bank below our house – fossicking for fallen almonds.

On the tree, almonds look like small green peaches, with fuzzy skins like worn tennis balls. When ready to pick, the skins split, revealing the hard-shelled nut inside. It's important to get that green husk off as soon as possible to prevent mould setting in, but judging precisely when to tackle that job is tricky. Pick too soon and the green flesh refuses to peel off cleanly; leave it too late and the nuts fall to the ground and the hulls harden and shrivel like shrink wrap.

Last autumn I picked 13 nuts; this year, 483. I've laid them out in wicker baskets under the eaves of the stables, out of reach of the dogs, so they can dry in the weak autumn sun. When they're ready to crack, the kernels rattle inside their shells. Fresh almonds are as sweet as marzipan and not at all like the barren specimens sold in plastic bags in the supermarket.

FRESH ALMONDS ARE AS SWEET AS MARZIPAN AND NOT AT ALL LIKE THE BARREN SPECIMENS SOLD IN THE SUPERMARKET

MAY 3: I can't fit any food in our fridge. It's crammed with bulging paper bags of spring bulbs. I've bought 300 tulips ('Purple Prince', 'New Design', 'Christmas Dream', 'Black Diamond' and 'Casablanca') and 150 hyacinths (50 each of lavender-pink 'Paul Herman', burgundy 'Woodstock' and indigo blue 'Peter Stuyvesant'). Giving them the cold shoulder for six to eight weeks snaps them out of their winter dormancy – mind you, we had a wicked early frost today, so I could just plant them.

Tulip bulbs

MAY 4: I must plant a noble persimmon tree – not for me, but for the tui. One tree is all I'd need, though a second variety improves fruit set. 'Fuyu' is the standard non-astringent commercial seller, but I could team it with early ripening 'Matsumoto Wase Fuyu' for a longer cropping season.

Not that I actually need to plant my own tree. My Aunty Bay's house is only 15 minutes from here and she's generous with the fruit from the persimmon at the edge of her deck. Known as 'the fruit of the gods', these decorative trees are one of the few to hold onto their fruit long after the leaves have fallen, giving the appearance of bare branches decorated with glowing orange baubles.

Aunty Bay doesn't eat any of her persimmons. She isn't a fan of their jellied texture and mellow flavour. She's content to let tui and bellbirds have their fill, then her free-range chooks clean up the hollowed carcasses as they plop onto the lawn.

Two years ago I sold 10kg of Aunty Bay's persimmons at the Hamilton Farmers' Market, for 50 cents each. By the close of trading, I had only six left, so I swapped them for a pack of sausages from Soggy Bottom Holdings. Jonathan and Sarah Walker are rare-breed pig farmers, with Tamworth, Large Black and Wessex Saddleback porkers. I'm going back to the Hamilton market later this month, on my first field day with the Franklin branch of the Tree Crops Association. I'll ask Jonathan if he has any piglets for sale.

PERSIMMON TREES ARE ONE OF THE FEW TO HOLD THEIR FRUIT LONG AFTER THE LEAVES HAVE FALLEN

Aunty Bay's 'Fuyu' persimmons

THERE ARE BITE MARKS IN
THE APPLES I LEFT IN A
BASKET ON THE DECK

MAY 8: When will I learn? There are bite marks in the apples I left in a basket on the deck and Mr Puppy Doo-Hawg, now far too mature for his name, is sporting a suspicious smirk.

I once tried to grow watercress on our deck. There's wild watercress in our stream so I hauled a clump out, flushed it clean (*Nasturtium officinale* absorbs contaminants like a vacuum cleaner) and urged it to prosper in a galvanised bucket. It was coming along nicely until the dog dragged it out one day, shook it like a dead duck, chewed the roots then downed the bucket of water.

Last autumn, Mr Puppy Doo-Hawg chewed through a 10-litre bucket of rugosa rosehips I'd collected to make rosehip syrup, having got all excited about its vitamin C content. When I found out I was expecting Lucas, Mum immediately produced my old Plunket book – she'd kept it safe in a suitcase for 37 years. My matronly Plunket nurse's name was Miss A and

Rugosa rosehips

Rosehip syrup

For the best flavour, harvest rosehips after the first winter frosts and be careful to strain out the tiny tickly hairs – they're the original source of itching powder. This recipe is adapted from 'The Hedgerow Harvest', a pamphlet issued in 1943 by Britain's Ministry of Food. The original recipe uses sugar but I prefer to use manuka honey. Roughly chop 500g rosehips in a food processor. Bring 1 litre of water to the boil in a pot; add hips and return to the boil. Remove from heat and steep, covered, for 30 minutes. Strain juice through a jelly bag or cheesecloth-lined sieve, then return pulp to the pot. Add 500ml extra boiling water; steep and strain again. Discard pulp. Pour juice into a small pot, simmer to reduce by half, then add 1 cup sugar or ½ cup manuka honey and boil for 5 minutes. Store in small, sterilised, dark glass bottles. Refrigerate after opening and use within a fortnight.

she'd advised Mum to administer a daily dose of vitamin C for good health, good teeth and a chirpy disposition (on my part).

Mum was encouraged to mix orange juice into my milk (not sure how she managed that, given that I was breastfed), feed me strained tamarillos or sieved kiwifruit (it was midwinter – nothing else was in season!) or add 5ml of rosehip syrup to a bottle of boiled water.

MAY 10: Last year we had an Indian summer that stretched into an Indian autumn, resulting in my best ever – and most surprising – crop of sweetcorn. I say surprising because I didn't sow it intending to eat any of it. I sowed it because I couldn't think of any other plant fast, tall or cheap enough to provide a lush backdrop behind the wildflower borders at our wedding.

I sourced bulk corn seed from a commercial seed merchant and Jason sowed 1200 seeds, three rows deep around the lawn and in blocks in the terraced beds below our house. He didn't sow by hand – hell no, it would have taken weeks – but pressed the seeds into the soil using my Uncle John's vintage one-wheeled push seeder, a natty gadget that carves a furrow, drops the seeds in at even intervals, then drags its chain to backfill the trench. It took 30 minutes to sow the lot.

Sowing corn at the end of December – at least six weeks later than any self-respecting gardening expert would advise – is foolhardy. Mine was only half a metre high by our mid-February wedding but I reckoned the cows would happily clean up the stalks after the ceremony. By then, however, I was six months pregnant and not particularly interested in pulling out 1200 tardy corn stalks, so I let it be. The mild weather can take the rest of the credit because, although sweetcorn is traditionally a summer crop, we were eating juicy corn on the cob until the end of May.

Figuring it was probably a fluke (but hoping it wasn't), I tried the same trick this year. On 29 December I sowed five packets of 'Chicago', a supersweet hybrid with kernels of honey and pearl, and a packet each of the heirloom varieties 'Hopi Blue' and 'Rainbow Inca'.

The coloured corns have come to nothing. My 'Hopi Blue', a flour corn that can be ground into flour to make nacho chips, is an insipid pale blue instead of the metallic black-purple it should be, while the kernels on the immature cobs of 'Rainbow Inca' are milky and faded rather than vibrant and multicoloured. Not that the cows complained – I fed them the whole crop.

As for 'Chicago'? I've filled the freezer and taken a crateful to the farmers' market, but I still can't keep up with all those juicy cobs. Plus we're going through a block of butter every week. If I repeat this exercise next autumn, I'd better get my hands on a placid house cow.

'Chicago' sweetcorn

MAY 12: For Mother's Day tomorrow, I've decided to make Mum and Maureen a trio of artisan almond treats: chocolate scorched almonds, honey roasted almonds, and cinnamon-encrusted almonds. But first I have to find a way to crack open the blimmin' shells.

There are two types of almonds; hard-shelled and soft- or paper-shelled. The soft-shelled types are easy to crack – their dry shells crumble under the merest pressure, offering easy access to the kernel – but the hard-shelled types are as solid as hand grenades. To hedge my bets, I planted a mix of both, including paper-shelled '403', 'IXL' and 'CY750', but all but eight of my nuts came from the hard-shelled 'Monovale' trees.

It took half an hour, and all my patience, to prise open the first dozen nuts. Jason came home to find me cursing in the kitchen, armed with a meat cleaver and a hammer. Google volunteered no miracle cure, though financial advisor and former Oregon state gubernatorial candidate Ed Winslow did send me in the right direction, via Yahoo.

'The easiest way for an individual to crack the shell and get to the prized nut inside is the way

---

Chocolate coated almonds

It's tricky to make smooth, shiny, oval scorched almonds without a candy mould. I, however, improvised and recycled the Mumi and Bubi trays I use to freeze puréed veges for Lucas. (Ice cube trays would also do the trick – who says scorched almonds can't have square corners?) Pre-roasting the almonds intensifies their flavour.

Method: Preheat oven to 160°C. Spread almonds in a single layer over a non-stick baking tray and roast for 10–15 minutes, shaking every few minutes. Remove from oven and set aside to cool. When the almonds are cool, melt a bar of good quality milk or dark chocolate in a bowl over a pot of simmering water. Take the chocolate off the heat and pop it in the fridge for a few minutes to cool (a process known as tempering), then reheat the chocolate. Spoon ½ teaspoon of melted chocolate into each mould, add an almond, then cover with more chocolate. Pop into the freezer; when cold, twist the tray and the chocolates should slip out without any trouble.

Honey roasted almonds

Roast 1 cup whole almonds for 10–15 minutes at 160°C. When the almonds are almost done, combine 2 tablespoons clear honey, 1 tablespoon water and 2 teaspoons cooking oil in a small saucepan. Bring to the boil, add almonds and cook for 2–3 minutes, stirring constantly. Be careful not to let the mixture burn.

Spoon almonds into a bowl, sprinkle with ¼ cup brown sugar and ½ teaspoon salt, and toss to coat. Spread over a non-stick tray lined with greaseproof paper to cool. For sweet, spiced nuts, add 1 teaspoon vanilla paste to the honey mixture and 1 teaspoon cinnamon to the sugar/salt to coat. Or, if you're feeling truly decadent, coat your honey roasted almonds in chocolate.

---

it's been done for years. Tools needed are a hammer and a hard surface. Almonds shells have a sharp edge and a round edge. Place the almond shell on the hard surface with the sharp edge up. Gently tap with the hammer progressively harder until the shell begins to crack. If done properly the shell will split into two halves with a snap and the almond nut will be there for the taking.'

I took Ed's advice. I took my basket of nuts out into the garden and, like a thrush shucking snails on a concrete patio, proceeded to smash my almonds against a solid half-tonne concrete lamp post that Jason had salvaged from a construction site. I soon had quite a rhythm going, reliably splitting each shell on the fourth or fifth crack.

Roasting the almonds will have to wait until tomorrow, though. I can barely raise my arm after all that bashing.

'Monovale' almonds

MAY 14: I've put a bottle of cider on ice. It's the final bottle from the last batch I made in the city, using apples foraged off a street tree around the corner from my cottage. (The fact that I still have a bottle of it reveals how much less explosive my 2010 vintage was than the fiercely fermentative plonk I produced in 2009.)

We'll drink it tonight. It seems appropriate. It has been two years to the day since I moved back to the land. For 731 days, I've felt at home on – or as near as possible to – the Hunua Ranges, halfway between Auckland's CBD and the farm where I grew up.

In that time, I got engaged, married, became a mum, signed up as a stallholder at the Clevedon Farmers' Market, taught my man how to make pasta and pavlova, brewed some pretty atrocious (and fairly ferocious) hop beer, learned how to drive a digger (we're ready to start excavating the 34 beds in my French formal garden) and, after 15 years of miserable, misshapen crops, finally conquered the carrot.

I'd like to say that my move back to the land was blissful from the very beginning but my insurance company would tell you otherwise. I'm always in a hurry – places to go, people to see, plants to acquire – and 14 May 2010, the day I moved to Hunua, was no different. I had a plane to catch, and not enough time to unpack. Jason and I were off to Taranaki, where I'd been invited to judge an heirloom pumpkin contest.

Mum offered to housesit (someone had to calm my agoraphobic cats, all three of which were cowering under the bed, too jittery to check out their new country digs) so we backed Jason's truck up to his shed, neatly stacked all my boxes into it, and headed off to New Plymouth. I boarded the flight with my de facto partner on one arm and – not to be outdone – a marvellous 15kg 'Musquee de Provence' pumpkin in the other.

I'm not the least bit superstitious but, as I stepped off the plane, I tripped and dropped my pumpkin. I heard it crack as it hit the tarmac and rolled down the runway. I could have cried, but I consoled myself with the knowledge that there were plenty more where it came from – 250kg more in fact, all safely curing in the tack room at one end of Jason's shed.

At 5a.m. the next morning, Jason's cellphone rang. It was my brother-in-law, Alan. 'Where are the keys to your car?' he asked. 'Why?' said Jason. 'Don't tell Lynda,' Alan sighed, 'but your shed's on fire and the car's about to go up next.'

At home in Hunua, a truck battery charger had arced in our shed, setting fire to the building and incinerating everything I owned, as well as all of Jason's tools, his motocross bike, surfboard, electric guitar and a chest freezer full of beef that had only just been delivered by Kev, the local homekill butcher.

I lost all my shoes, my heirloom seeds (that'll teach me for stockpiling instead of sowing), the spring bulbs I hadn't got around to planting, a dozen handblown glass paperweights and 38 pieces of retro Anchor Hocking Fairfield avocado green glassware from the 1970s (I was only one dinner plate and a wine goblet short of completing my collection, courtesy of eBay). I lost a library's worth of gardening books – from

> # OF ALL THE THINGS I LOST NONE PEEVED ME MORE THAN THE UNTIMELY COMBUSTION OF ALL MY PRESERVES FROM THE PREVIOUS SUMMER

encyclopaedias to coffee-table compendiums – and every cookbook I owned, bar one. Mum's trusty batter-splattered *Edmonds Cookery Book* escaped the flames because, as luck would have it, I'd put it in my handbag the day before because I wanted to bake a banana cake.

On the bright side, Mum got a ripping yarn to recount to her golfing mates, the local volunteer fire brigade had a blast putting out the blaze and no one was hurt, unless you count my pumpkins. They were all roasted whole.

I suspect it was a blessing that I wasn't there to watch my old life go up in flames, though the experience ultimately proved quite cathartic. (Unlike, say, one of my friend's attempts to expunge a particularly hurtful relationship breakup by setting fire to her ex-boyfriend's letters. Without a fireplace to fling them into, she ceremonially flicked a lighter at each page and watched the words turn to ash in a roasting dish on the floor. Out of sight, out of mind . . . At least that was the theory. Unfortunately the roasting dish got so hot it melted the carpet, costing her the tenancy bond and leaving a singed mark to remind her, daily, of her lost love.)

I didn't cry (much). I composted my barbecued gardening books, made a mosaic out of my broken plates, fed the pumpkins to the chooks – I've never seen such golden yolks – and started my new life in the country with a clean slate, not to mention a surprisingly tidy house. (At least until the insurance payout came through, at which point I started cluttering it up again.)

Of all the things I lost in that fire, none peeved me more than the untimely combustion of all my preserves from the previous summer: 30 jars of 'Damson' plum jam, half a dozen jars of boysenberry jam, some courgette and apple chutney and a dozen pint jars packed with Central Otago cherries in brandy. The jam turned to blackened toffee, the rubber seals melted off the pickle jars and the brandy evaporated in the heat, leaving the smoke-contaminated cherries high and dry.

This year, I'm taking no chances. I'm not letting my preserves out of my sight. They're safely stacked in the pantry and on shelves in our lounge, where I can stare at them with smug satisfaction.

In 1939, in her first year of life as a country wife, Grandma filled her pantry with bottled tomatoes and nectarines, apple jelly and salted beans. She made dozens of jars of jam – plum, peach, gooseberry and strawberry, for starters – and foraged for wild blackberries.

In my first year as a country wife, I haven't done too badly either. I feel so blessed to be back on the land and, despite the many challenges of country gardening – possums, pukekos, foraging pheasants, egg-snatching dogs, Houdini heifers and a husband who can't be trusted with petrol-powered hedge trimmers – this really is the good life.

I want for nothing except, perhaps, a heated glasshouse so I can grow blight-free tomatoes, a top-notch rotary hoe, a pedigree pair of shaggy Highland cattle . . . and a new shed in which to store my preserves.

Better make that a new shed fitted with a smoke alarm.

END-OF-SEASON STOCKTAKE

My grandmothers' cupboards were never bare. With large families to feed – and no chest freezers in which to store their excess crops – they filled their pantries with jars of pickles and preserved fruit. They were far too busy to conduct an end-of-season stocktake. (As a growing boy, my Dad worked this fact to his advantage; he stole a quart jar of peaches every week, ate the evidence in one go, then rinsed the jar and carefully slid it to the back of the shelf with all the other empties. Grandma was never any the wiser.)

Although I only have three mouths to feed, one thing's for sure: we won't starve in winter . . . and Jason won't be able to help himself, because I've counted every jar.

Bottled beverages: 'Damson' plum gin, 2 litres; elderberry cordial, 1 bottle; feijoa wine, 6 bottles; hop beer, 12 bottles; lemon cordial, 3 bottles; rhubarb champagne, 2 bottles; rhubarb wine, 6 bottles; quince vodka, 2 litres; strawberry liqueur, 1 bottle.

Bottled fruit: apples, 6 jars; apricots, 16 jars; cherries, 3 jars; nectarines, 1 jar; passionfruit pulp, 5 jars; peacherines, 3 jars; peaches, 5 jars; pears, 14 jars; plums, 17 jars; quinces, 5 jars.

Chutneys, pickles and sauces: apple sauce, 14 jars; apple and elderberry sauce, 4 jars; elderberry sauce, 1 jar; pickled onions, 8 jars; quince chutney, 4 jars; tomato and plum sauce, 4 bottles.

Jams and jellies: apricot jam, 2 jars; 'Blackboy' peach jam, 4 jars; boysenberry jam, 3 jars; 'Damson' plum jam, 16 jars; elderberry and plum jam, 4 jars; quince jam, 1 jar; quince jelly, 3 jars; strawberry jam, 3 jars.

Seeds saved: capucijner peas, 1kg; crimson-flowered broad beans, 160 seeds; garlic, 72 bulbs; peas, 1 pint jar; poppy seeds, 1 pint jar.

Vegetables, fresh: Brussels sprouts; cauliflowers; cavolo nero; celeriac; chillies; leeks; lettuce; sweetcorn.

Vegetables, stored: beans, 2 jars bottled and 2kg frozen; corn, 5kg frozen; potatoes, 17kg; pumpkin, 15kg; tomatoes, 20 jars.

A FEW OF MY FAVOURITE THINGS

GARDENING TOOLS: I wouldn't be without my Fiskars secateurs (I have about six pairs because I'm always losing them) and, because my husband has made a habit of snapping the ends off cheaper forks and spades, he has a set of Fiskars long-handled, heavy-duty ergonomic tools – a fork, spade and shovel. My Burgon & Ball fruit picker (available from The Company Shed) makes it easier, if still not exactly easy, to harvest the highest pears and, when planting out seedlings I use the vintage-styled Joseph Bentley range of wooden-handled hand forks and trowels, just because I like the look of them. Gubba Trugs are essential for carting compost and heavy crops – or fill them with weeds, cover with water and leave to rot down to make a bucket of liquid fertiliser.

JOIN THE CLUB: Gardening clubs and societies are a rich resource – and a great place to source heirloom seeds and spare cuttings. I'm a member of the Heritage Rose Society (**www.heritageroses.org.nz**), the Ararimu branch of the Country Women's Institute (**www.wi.org.nz**) and the Tree Crops Association (**www.treecrops.org.nz**). *NZ Gardener*'s website (**www.nzgardener.co.nz**) includes a comprehensive list of local gardening clubs and specialist horticultural societies.

BOOKS: Whenever I have a glut of fruit or vegetables to get through, I return time and again to Nigel Slater's *Tender Volume I* and *Tender Volume II* (recently reprinted as *Ripe*). Nigel Slater can make even silverbeet sound sexy, and his recipes are scrummy. Stephanie Alexander's *Kitchen Garden Companion* is also helpfully divided into crops and their culinary uses. I devour anything by Hugh Fearnley-Whittingstall but *River Cottage Veg Everyday!*

gets the nod ahead of the rest because, though 100 per cent vegetarian, it's refreshingly light on lentils. And Darina Allen's *Forgotten Skills of Cooking* is a wonderful resource for country cooks and farm gardeners – should I ever need to truss a goose, fry comfrey fritters or brew nettle beer, I know where to turn for advice.

GET GROWING: Every Friday, I write *NZ Gardener's* weekly online magazine *Get Growing* – it's packed with weekend tasks, competitions, harvest recipes and how-to advice for vege gardens and home orchards. To subscribe, email **getgrowing@nzgardener.co.nz**

ONLINE RESOURCES: For vegetable, flower and herb seeds (both heirloom and modern hybrids), see the online catalogues at **www.kingsseeds. co.nz** and **www.egmontseeds.co.nz**

I order vege and flower seedlings from Awapuni Nurseries in Palmerston North. They're great value and, as they come wrapped in newspaper in recycled cardboard cartons, there's no plastic rubbish – and they only charge $4 for rural delivery if you order six bundles or more. See **www.awapuni.co.nz**

For hand-crafted wooden trugs, gorgeous Kiwi-made gardening accessories, seeds, fruit trees and general advice for living the good life, Heather Cole has it covered at Mapua Country Trading, on the wharf at Mapua or at **www.mapuacountrytrading.co.nz**

Keen on home brewing? For fermenting vessels, wine yeast and airlocks, see **www.brewcraft.co.nz**. And if you can turn it into booze, you'll find a recipe at **winemaking. jackkeller.net**

Sarah Frater has an appetising selection of mail-order fruit trees, including the Koanga heirloom collection, at **www.ediblegarden.co.nz**

For groovy kitchen gadgets, such as chef's gas torches and ice cream machines, order from **www.millyskitchen.co.nz**

For pickling and preserving, order jars from Arthur Holmes in Wellington, **www.arthurholmes.co.nz**

Nicole Smith at The Company Shed, **www.thecompanyshed.co.nz**, sells cloches, fruit pickers, seed boxes and other accessories.

For wildflower seeds and a wide range of mail-order plants and bulbs, see **www.gardenpost.co.nz**

For heirloom tomatoes, Bristol Seeds in Whanganui has hundreds of varieties to choose from **www.bristol.co.nz**

Waimea Nurseries supply fruit trees to garden centres; though a wholesaler, their website is a handy resource for researching the best varieties: **www.waimeanurseries.co.nz**

If you love old roses (and who doesn't?), then peruse the online catalogues at Tasman Bay Roses, **www.tbr.co.nz**, and Trinity Farm, **www.trinityfarm.co.nz**

For gladioli, lilies, tulips and other gorgeous bulbs, see **www.nzbulbs.co.nz**

For dazzling dahlias (and an amazing display garden), **www.dahliahaven.co.nz**

Join the Koanga Institute, **www.koanga.org.nz**, to help save New Zealand's heritage food crops; Kay Baxter's fruit trees and seeds are also stocked by Kaiwaka Organics, **www.kaiwakaorganics.co.nz**

To garden by the moon, order a $5 instructional calendar from Robert Guyton at the South Coast Environment Society in Riverton, **www.sces.org.nz**

Support your local farmers' market (and plan holiday itineraries) – you'll find locations and opening times listed at **www.farmersmarket.org.nz**

My blog is **www.lyndahallinan.com**

ACKNOWLEDGEMENTS

People often say to me, 'I don't know how you do it all!', but the simple truth is that I don't. This book would never have progressed past the pages of scrawled notes in my garden diary were it not for my mum, my mother-in-law Maureen and Melissa Mooney, who took it in turns to keep Lucas amused – I've never heard so many rousing renditions of 'Old MacDonald Had a Farm' – as I was sequestered indoors writing about everything that was going on outdoors.

Thanks are also due to my husband Jason, who turned a blind eye to the screeds of paper that eventually covered every square centimetre of our bedroom floor. I suspect by now he has realised that my domestic skills are limited to cooking and growing; I'm yet to master cleaning or sewing. Actually, I'm yet to master weeding also. I relied on Nicola Hinton, my husband's cousin's wife and the hardest-working landscape gardener in the northern Waikato, to keep my garden ticking over (and weed-free) in the weeks before and after Lucas was born.

If a picture tells a thousand words then this book is not mine but Sally Tagg's. Sally and I have worked together for over 15 years and every minute has been an absolute pleasure (and not just because we're usually on a sugar high, stuffing down trifle and crème brûlée or knocking back home-brewed booze). Sally, you are an artist in every sense of the word – even my black-spot-blighted 'Granny Smith' apples look beautiful – and it's a privilege to have you as a friend.

That is true, too, of Julian Matthews, former editor of *NZ Gardener* and my mentor in both horticulture and publishing. Julian somehow escaped mention in this book, largely because he prefers dramatic foliage to food crops, but my time working as his deputy shaped both my career and my all-consuming passion for plants.

My colleagues at Fairfax Magazines have been a great support and no one said a thing about all the meetings I missed while writing this book.

Thank you especially to Lynley, for agreeing to let me work from the wops; to Rachel, for always being such a willing accomplice; and to Olivia, for all those last-minute design favours, from wedding invitations to Foggydale Farm labels for at the market. Speaking of Foggydale Farm, it has never looked as good as it does on illustrator extraordinaire Chris Mousdale's marvellous map on page 16. If only there really was a dinosaur skulking in our swamp . . .

Living in a rural community is anything but isolating. All the time I used to spend sitting in congested traffic I now spend gasbagging to fellow gardeners and growers on the blower. People like Nadene Hall, the effervescent editor of *NZ Lifestyle Block* magazine, Robert Guyton in Riverton, Gerard Martin at Kings Seeds, Heather Cole at Mapua Country Trading, and Sheryn Clothier, who edits the Tree Crops Association's journal. (And as the Tree Crops Association's official patron, I implore you to join us – you'll never meet a more enthusiastic bunch to learn from.)

When I moved to Hunua, Mike and Jackie Julian welcomed me with open arms, open bottles of bubbles and emergency truckloads of water, while Helen Dorresteyn invited me to join the Clevedon Farmers' Market community – and what fun it has been getting to know all the other likeminded local growers.

I'm a shameless scrumper – of feijoas, elderberries and other people's recipes – so thanks to Ray McVinnie, Kelda Hains, Helen Jackson, Paul Jobin, Beki Lamb, Celia Harvey, Shelly Jiang, and Alison Worth for generously sharing yours.

And last but not least, thank you to Debra Millar, Catherine O'Loughlin, Caroline Budge, Sarah Healey, Raewyn Davies and the rest of the team at Penguin, for being patient and unfailingly polite, even though this book took longer to germinate than a packet of stale parsnip seeds.

Jason's cat, imaginatively named Cat

Cook's Index

Gardener's Index

Image credits

t = top
b = bottom
c = centre
l = left
r = right

Photography copyright © as listed below

Lynda Hallinan
pages 20 (bl, tr), 23 (tl, br), 25 (r), 26-27, 28 (b), 33 (t), 36 (bl), 43 (tl, br), 48, 50, 52, 57 (tr), 58 (l, tr, br), 59, 60, 64 (b), 66, 70 (tc), 72-75, 77, 78 (tr), 81-85, 89 (tl, tr, br), 94, 97, 98 (tr), 100, 103, 104 (tl, br), 105, 106, 108, 109 (br), 110 (l, c), 111 (c), 113 (c, r), 115, 124 (bc), 126, 128, 134 (t,b), 135 (bl), 138 (tl, tr), 147, 149, 150 (tl, bl), 153, 154, 160 (tl), 161, 165, 169 (t), 176 (tc), 180, 185, 193 (l), 196, 200 (tr), 207, 209, 212 (r), 214-215, 216 (l), 220, 224, 225, 227, 228 (t), 237 (b), 243

Sally Tagg/Penguin
pages 2-7, 18-19, 20 (tl, br), 22, 23 (tc, tr, bl, bc), 24, 25 (l), 30-32, 33 (b), 34-35, 36 (tl, tc, tr, bc, br), 38, 39 (t), 40-41, 43 (tr, bl), 44-46, 49, 51, 54-55, 57 (tl, tc, bl, br), 58 (cr), 61, 63, 64 (t), 65, 67, 68-69, 70 (tl, tr, bl, bc, br), 78 (l, br), 79-80, 86, 89 (bl), 90-93, 95, 98 (br), 99, 101, 104 (tr, bl), 107, 109 (tl, tr, bl), 110 (r), 111 (l, r), 112, 113 (l), 116-121, 122,123, 124 (tl, tc, bl), 127 (tl, tr, bl), 129 (t,b), 134 (tl, br), 138 (tc, bl, bc, br), 140-145, 146 (b), 148, 150 (r), 151, 155, 168, 169 (b), 172-173, 174-175, 176 (tl, tr, bc, br), 182-183, 187, 188-192, 193 (r), 200 (tl, bl, br), 202-203, 206, 208, 210, 211 (l), 212 (l, c), 213, 216 (r), 221, 222, 229-236, 237 (t), 238-239, 245-247

Sally Tagg/*NZ Gardener*
pages 28 (t), 39 (b), 76, 124 (tr, bl), 127 (br), 130-131, 132-133, 135 (tr), 136-367, 146 (t), 152, 156-159, 160 (tr), 162, 164, 166, 169 (c), 170-171, 176 (bl), 178-179, 181, 184, 186, 195, 197, 199, 204-205, 211 (c, r), 217, 218, 223, 226, 228 (b), 240

Howard Small
page 13

Geoff Osborne
page 15

PENGUIN BOOKS
Published by the Penguin Group
Penguin Group (NZ), 67 Apollo Drive, Rosedale,
Auckland 0632, New Zealand (a division of Pearson New Zealand Ltd)
Penguin Group (USA) Inc., 375 Hudson Street,
New York, New York 10014, USA
Penguin Group (Canada), 90 Eglinton Avenue East, Suite 700, Toronto,
Ontario, M4P 2Y3, Canada (a division of Pearson Penguin Canada Inc.)
Penguin Books Ltd, 80 Strand, London, WC2R 0RL, England
Penguin Ireland, 25 St Stephen's Green,
Dublin 2, Ireland (a division of Penguin Books Ltd)
Penguin Group (Australia), 250 Camberwell Road, Camberwell,
Victoria 3124, Australia (a division of Pearson Australia Group Pty Ltd)
Penguin Books India Pvt Ltd, 11, Community Centre,
Panchsheel Park, New Delhi – 110 017, India
Penguin Books (South Africa) (Pty) Ltd, Block D, Rosebank Office Park,
181 Jan Smuts Avenue, Parktown North, Gauteng 2193, South Africa

Penguin Books Ltd, Registered Offices: 80 Strand, London, WC2R 0RL,
England

First published by Penguin Group (NZ), 2012
10 9 8 7 6 5 4 3 2 1

Copyright © Lynda Hallinan, 2012

The right of Lynda Hallinan to be identified as the author of this work in
terms of section 96 of the Copyright Act 1994 is hereby asserted.

Designed and typeset by Sarah Healey, © Penguin Group (NZ)
Map on pages 16–17 by Chris Mousdale
Prepress by Image Centre Ltd
Printed in China by 1010 Printing

ISBN 978-0-143-56708-0

A catalogue record for this book is available
from the National Library of New Zealand.

www.penguin.co.nz